DEVON TOWN TRAILS

EXETER
AND EAST DEVON

Compiled by Peter Hunt and Marilyn Wills

DEVON BOOKS

ACKNOWLEDGEMENTS

The publishers wish to thank the following for kindly providing photographs:

Exeter City Museums Archaeological Field Unit
Express and Echo/Western Times Co. Ltd.
Royal Commission on the Historical Monuments of England
Dr D. J. C. Laming
Dr A. Jennings
Mr J. Berry
Mr T. Jones
Mr P. J. Hunt
Mr J. Yallop
Mr C. Bowerman

Drawing of Roman legionary fortress by E. Kadow
Maps by Ian Foulis and Associates

First published in Great Britain in 1988 by Devon Books

This book was compiled by Peter J. Hunt, Amenities and Countryside Officer of the Property Department of Devon County Council, on behalf of the Amenities and Countryside Committee. Director of Property is Andrew Smy.

ISBN: 0 86114–812–6

British Library Cataloguing-in-Publication Data

Exeter and East Devon.— (Devon town trails).
1. Devon – Walkers' guides
I. Hunt, P.J. (Peter John), *1935*–   II. Wills,
Marilyn   III. Series
914.23′504858

Printed and bound in Great Britain by A. Wheaton & Co. Ltd.

DEVON BOOKS
Official Publisher to Devon County Council
An Imprint of Wheaton Publishers Ltd, a Maxwell Communication Corporation plc Company.
Hennock Road, Marsh Barton, Exeter, Devon EX2 8RP
Tel: 0392 74121; Telex 42749 (WHEATN G)

SALES
Direct sales enquiries to Devon Books at the address above.

Trade sales to: Town & Country Books, P.O. Box 31, Newton Abbot, Devon TQ12 5AQ. Tel: 080 47 2690

PREFACE

Devon's long and varied history is better written in the buildings of its towns and villages than in textbooks of national repute. Although every community is touched by the events that determine a nation's destiny, it is the local trials, tragedies and eccentricities, remembered in the market-place and often forgotten as quickly as they occur, which are the important daily fare of those whose lives make history's generalities. Obscure lives lived in remote villages and towns still leave their own records in the buildings and hedgerows, and even prehistoric rites affect the landscape, although the lives of those who built the tumuli (like those in Farway Parish, close to the A375 Honiton to Sidmouth road) have long been lost in time.

Each town and village has a mosaic of history within it; the habits and limitations of each era leave their mark, arising perhaps from the eccentricities of the builder or a peculiarly local requirement. Local building materials used by traditional craftsmen give different places in Devon a different 'feel' and a charm of their own. In East Devon there is great variety; in Exeter the ancient walls of the city are built of local red sandstone whilst its eighteenth-century terraces with pink brick and slate roofs are warmly attractive. Cob and thatch pervades the whole area, but at Colyton, for example, flint is used, and Beer stone, found in windows of ancient farmhouses throughout East Devon, is common in buildings at Beer, whilst Axminster has its own yellow-brown limestone.

If the individual styles of the buildings are fascinating, the lives and fortunes of those who lived in them are equally interesting. Sometimes great events that shook the country, like the Monmouth Rebellion of 1685, had a particular importance for East Devon. Monmouth's followers came from all over East Devon although Axminster, Colyton and Honiton contributed more than most, and in the course of time Judge Jeffreys came to Colyton to dispense justice. He stayed in one of the attractive cob-and-thatch buildings that still make it one of the most pleasant spots in this part of Devon.

Over a century later the Napoleonic Wars provided the springboard of change for almost every aspect of the county's life, and signalled the expansion and increased popularity of a number of seaside towns and villages. Exmouth had already started to grow as a holiday resort in the 1760s, and had attracted Lady Byron and Lady Nelson to live at the Beacon. Sidmouth drew nobility to its shore and its popularity with the well-to-do and famous helped to create one of the finest Regency resorts in the country. Budleigh Salterton grew in the early nineteenth century and like Sidmouth retains its superior quality whilst Seaton, further east along the coast, reflects the coming of the railway and holidays for all.

Each town and village has its ghosts and an atmosphere of its own. Invariably the character of Devon's towns is felt in the ancient streets and buildings of their centres. In the past it has often been the local people who have had to protect the old town centres from those who would destroy them for either profit or convenience, and in this respect have been more effective and sensitive than local authorities. It is appropriate that the representatives of conservation and amenity societies should have produced new guides to their towns and villages to share their own pride and knowledge of them with all who are interested. This initiative has been encouraged by the Amenities and Countryside Committee of Devon County Council and reflects the growing concern of everyone to keep the most attractive areas from unnecessary change. It would be impossible to recapture the quaint charm that their courtyards and alleys give to Lympstone or Topsham, or the dignity of Regency and early Victorian terraces found all over East Devon, and the descriptions in this volume rightly emphasize this.

Peter Hunt

CONTENTS

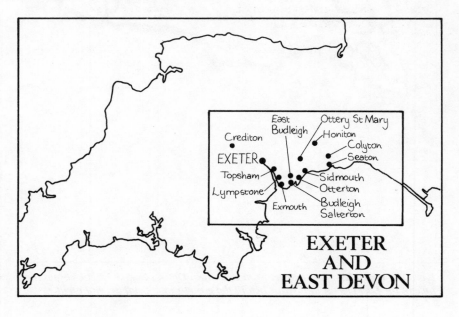

EXETER
AND
EAST DEVON

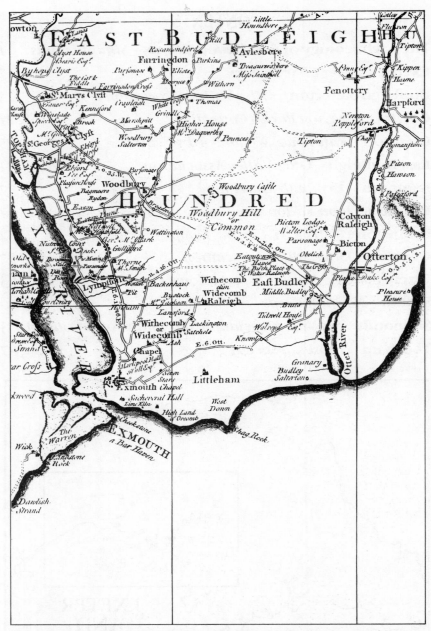

East Devon in 1765. This extract from Benjamin Donn's Map of Devon *shows the face of the East Devon landscape before the growth in coastal development.*

THE ARCHAEOLOGY OF EAST DEVON TOWNS

For many visitors to the towns of East Devon, the most obvious signs of their historic past are the many attractive old buildings lining the main streets. However, the shops and houses we see today form but the latest layer in the build-up of urban life that has been going on since medieval times. Apart from the medieval parish churches, few urban buildings more than 400 years old survive to this day. This is due in part to the rapid changes caused by development over the past thirty years, but earlier centuries have also taken their toll. The houses of Axminster were almost totally destroyed during the Civil War and towns such as Crediton and Honiton suffered terrible fires in the eighteenth century. Thus if we wish to follow the story of the origin and earlier growth of towns in East Devon we need to look beyond their historic buildings and see what archaeology can tell us about a town's past.

The origins of towns in East Devon

Urban life in East Devon can be traced back some 1900 years to Roman times. Following the conquest of 43 A.D. the Romans established a fortress at Exeter and this grew into *Isca Dumnoniorum*, the capital city of the Roman South-West. The line of the Roman town walls at Exeter can still be walked today and Exeter remains our only certain Roman town in Devon. Traces of smaller Roman settlements have however been found in other East Devon towns such as Exmouth, Seaton and Topsham, whilst Honiton and Axminster lie astride the main Roman road to Exeter and the West.

Our knowledge of urban life in East Devon during the Saxon period is very limited. Axminster, Crediton, Exeter and Ottery St Mary were important ecclesiastical centres and a fine Saxon cross has been found at Colyton. However, Exeter is the only East Devon town documented in the years leading up to the Norman Conquest of 1066 and it is the only one to be recorded as a borough in the great Domesday survey of 1086.

According to Domesday Book, there was also a market at Otterton in 1086 and it was the need for regulated market centres that led to the creation of a host of medieval towns and boroughs over the next 300 years. There were about a hundred market towns in Devon in the Middle Ages and East Devon with its rich farmlands had over thirty. They ranged from important boroughs such as Axminster, Crediton and Exeter which had (and still have) large weekly markets, to modest market towns serving their local farming communities. Some of these small towns have long since shrunk back to villages whilst a few have completely disappeared from the map.

Most of our modern town centres have their origins as borough towns in the Middle Ages but some are relative newcomers. In East Devon this is particularly true of the coastal settlements. In earlier times, the coasts were exposed to enemy attack and places such as East Budleigh, Lympstone, Seaton and even Exmouth were little more than fishing villages until the eighteenth century, when they began to be popular as holiday resorts.

To date, archaeologists have been able to carry out very little excavation in the towns of East Devon apart from Exeter. Recent rescue work in advance of the redevelopment of Exmouth town centre has shown how investigation can reveal more of a town's early history, but for the time being much of our understanding of the way towns have grown must be derived from studying their historic town plans.

The historic plans of East Devon towns

The art of town planning is by no means a recent discovery. Exeter, like other Roman towns, had a regular layout of streets and we can see examples of deliberate medieval town planning in many of the East Devon towns. Despite the changes of the last thirty years, historic town plans, some dating back nearly 800 years, can still be traced today. The understanding of these historic town plans can add to the interest of a visit to any town. Among the features of the historic plan, the following are some to look for:

1. *Situation*
   Medieval towns often grew up at the junction of well-used roads or at a river crossing. Thus Axminster lies close to the junction of two main Roman roads and also at a crossing of the Axe. Exeter occupies a similar strategic position at the lowest bridging-point on the River Exe whilst, further north, Thorverton lies beside a crossing of the Exe and on the old cross-country route linking the two medieval boroughs of Crediton and Bradninch.

2. *Market-places*
   The weekly market was the focus of town life in the Middle Ages and this is reflected in the large market-places which accommodated the stalls, animal pens and other temporary market fixtures. In some towns the market was held in a central square. Often these squares have been partially infilled with small groups of houses but their

original outline can still be traced. In other towns the market was simply held in the main street and this accounts for the exceptional width of some main streets today. Honiton, Cullompton and Crediton are good examples of this and an eighteenth-century plan of Crediton shows the individual market buildings and fittings which occupied the centre of the High Street before the great fire of 1743.

3. *Street patterns and property boundaries*
Many medieval market towns grew up on the site of older villages and hamlets, which did not have any regular layout of streets and properties. However, the acquisition of urban status often brought with it the deliberate remodelling of the old plan, and the regular layout of medieval town centres is even more apparent with the new towns, which were laid out on open ground.

These new towns were commonly laid out on main roads to take advantage of passing trade and there are good examples in East Devon at Honiton, Newton Poppleford and Colyford. Honiton was created by the Earl of Devon in the late twelfth century and laid out on the old Roman road well away from the parish church. The regular town plan consisted of side lanes running at right angles from the main street and the property boundaries followed the same pattern. These town properties, known as 'burgage plots', had narrow frontages to the main street and ran back a considerable distance to a back lane. In this way every occupant had a street frontage from which to trade. Rather suprisingly this pattern of long narrow town properties still survives in parts of most medieval towns.

4. *Industrial areas*
Just as today industrial estates are built away from residential areas, so in the Middle Ages areas of industrial activity were often concentrated in a particular part of a town. In many instances this location was determined by access to a good water supply, to power mills and for other industrial purposes, and this was particularly true in the towns which were active in the woollen cloth trade. This was a major industry in medieval Devon, involving Exeter and major towns like Crediton as well as smaller East Devon settlements such as Axminster, Cullompton and Uffculme.

Historic towns have remained centres of industry through to modern times and they still contain some fine examples of nineteenth-century industrial buildings. These may not be as attractive to the eye as other historic buildings but they are just as much a part of the story of a town's past, which can be discovered by the visitor following the trails described in this book.

Simon Timms,
Archaeological Officer, Devon County Council Property Department   3

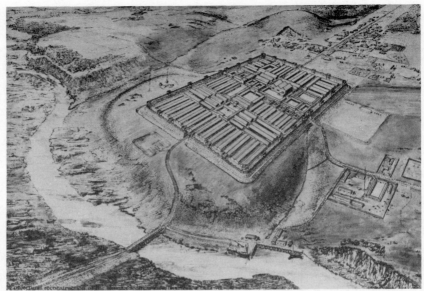

Roman legionary fortress at Exeter. This artist's reconstruction gives an idea of the size and layout of the fortress which was constructed by the Roman army on the banks of the Exe over 1900 years ago.

The medieval town plan of Cullompton, with its long narrow burgage plots at right angles to the main street, is clearly visible in this aerial view. Note how the main street bows out at one end. This was the medieval open market-place.

The old brush works, Castle Street, Axminster. The East Devon towns were centres of industry from the Middle Ages onwards. Old industrial buildings such as this one do much to give a town its character. This archive photograph was taken in 1948.

Exeter city walls follow the original Roman town wall line. Here they have been breached by the modern inner bypass.

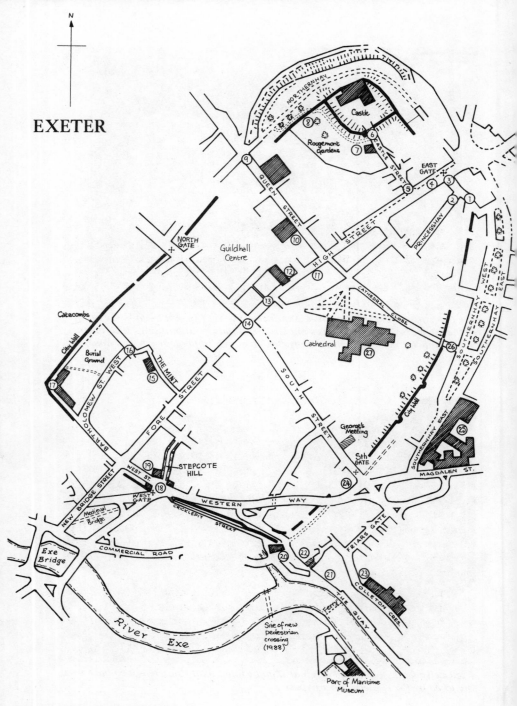

EXETER

N

Castle

Rougemont
Gardens

NORTHERNHAY

CASTLE STREET

EAST
GATE

Guildhall
Centre

QUEEN STREET

HIGH STREET

NORTH
GATE

PRINCESSHAY

WEST
EAST

SOUTHERNHAY

Catacombs

City Wall

Burial
Ground

THE MINT

ST. WEST

FORE STREET

BARTHOLOMEW

SOUTH STREET

Cathedral

CATHEDRAL CLOSE

City Wall

SOUTHERNHAY EAST

George's
Meeting

Sth
GATE

STEPCOTE
HILL

WEST ST.

WEST
GATE

MAGDALEN ST.

NEW BRIDGE STREET

Medieval
Bridge

WESTERN WAY

CRICKLEPIT STREET

Exe
Bridge

COMMERCIAL ROAD

FRIARS GATE

THE QUAY

COLLETON CRES.

River Exe

Site of new
pedestrian
crossing
(1988)

Parc of Maritime
Museum

Updated by Exeter Civic Society June 1987

EXETER

A Walk around Exeter City

Much of the long and chequered history of Exeter can be read in its buildings. Although little remains above ground of the Roman and medieval cities, archaeological finds are being made every year that enlarge our knowledge of Exeter's history. This guide deals with what can be seen in an afternoon's walk around the historic heart of the city, especially the rich variety of buildings from the mid-fifteenth century to the 1980s, following very approximately the route of the ancient city walls.

Start at the north-east end of Princesshay, at the entrance to the **Underground Passages (1)**, which were part of Exeter's medieval water supply system. Look around: although you are surrounded by modern buildings (mostly 1955–60), evidence of the past is plentiful. The post-war pedestrian street of **Princesshay (2)** is aligned on the twelfth-century towers of the cathedral; to the east you will see a corner tower of the city wall, which stretches away down Southernhay. The wall, which defended the city for nearly 1500 years, began as a Roman bank in A.D. 120; the wall itself was built in A.D. 200, repaired by King Athelstan in 928, greatly strengthened by 1066 but subsequently fell into great disrepair. It had four large gates, though all were demolished to make way for increased traffic between 1769 and 1819. Facing the High Street, you will see a band of crazy paving which marks the line of the city wall as far as the stone on the site of the **East Gate (3)** (also see the plaque in the pavement).

Turn left along the **High Street (4)**, here completely rebuilt after wartime bomb damage, and cross over to **Castle Street (5)**, at the top of which is the site of Exeter Castle, built by order of William the Conqueror in 1068. The Assize Courts were built in the centre of the Castle in 1774, and the buildings now house the Crown Court. Facing Castle Street is the impressive **Norman gatehouse (6)**, which once had a drawbridge, and the triangular window-heads probably mean that they were built by Saxon craftsmen.

Turn left into Rougemont Gardens, which were laid out in the eighteenth-century in the outer bailey of the castle; the great castle ditch is a prominent feature of the gardens. **Rougemont House (7)** on the left, built in 1769 with nineteenth-century additions, is a Museum of Costume and Lace. Follow the path along the castle wall until you reach the city wall: here a small gate **(8)** leads into **Northernhay Gardens**, but note, before you pass through, the herringbone pattern of stonework of the wall itself which shows it to be of Roman construction. To the right is Athelstan's tower, where castle and city walls meet.

Through the wall, look right at the fine war memorial; the pleasant gardens give a view of the Longbrook valley, long ago filled with railway, and note the outer face of the wall with its several ages of repair. Turn left to **Queen Street (9)** and note the Exeter Dispensary on the corner with Northernhay Street, and Exeter Central Station to the right which was rebuilt in 1933. Queen Street is a wide thoroughfare superimposed on the medieval street plan in 1835, with many imposing Victorian public buildings including the neoclassical Higher Market (1838) and the neo-Gothic Royal Albert Memorial Museum (1865) with its great variety of building stone. The Higher Market has been restored and now forms part of a modern shopping precinct, clustered around St Pancras' Church; opposite is the Old Post Office Building with a top-heavy façade and central alleyway leading to Gandy Street (now pedestrianized and worth a small detour). Beyond the market, the imposing Victorian-style façade **(10)** is a reconstruction of a former building, demolished in 1980; on top, the statue of Queen Victoria is a fibreglass replica of an earlier one.

At the end of Queen Street, rejoin the High Street and notice a number of timber-framed merchants' houses of the sixteenth and seventeenth centuries, especially **41–42 High Street (11)** (1564) where some of the interior decoration survives. Walk down the High Street to the **Guildhall (12)**, the oldest municipal building in the country still in regular use as a council-chamber. There has been a building here since 1160 but the present building is largely fifteenth to sixteenth century; the Renaissance portico reflects the wealth generated in the sixteenth century by the wool trade. The interior is well worth a visit. Opposite, beside Broadgate, is the old City Bank, an imposing Palladian-style building in Bath stone (1875–7).

From the High Street, note the variety of street widths: Martin's Lane, opposite Queen Street, and Broadgate, are both rather narrow entries into Cathedral Yard; the gate structure of the latter was demolished in 1825 to ease the flow of traffic. Opposite Broadgate is **Parliament Street (13)**, which is believed to be the narrowest street in the world and contrasts with broad Queen Street – the names possibly reflect Exeter city's affiliations in the Civil War!

A timber-framed merchant's house in Exeter High Street, now a shop

At the **Carfax (14)**, four ancient main streets still meet as they did in Roman times: Fore Street and High Street, North Street and South Street. Many of the buildings are post-war, but note the brick, stone and terracotta building (1907) on the north corner: a statue of St Peter which once stood on the façade was found to be 700 years old, and is due to be replaced with a fibreglass replica. The original will be found in the Museum in Queen Street.

Walk down Fore Street to The Mint, a narrow medieval street leading to **St Nicholas' Priory (15)** (1080); the surviving guest wing with its fascinating interior is open to the public, and beside it is a new Peace Garden. Further along, The Mint issues into **Bartholomew Street (16)**, the leafy spaciousness of the former burial ground of Friernhay contrasting pleasantly with the closeness of the central area. Carpenter Close (St Wilfred's), a sheltered housing scheme overlooking the green, is an outstanding blend of modern and period architecture and has two award plaques.

Walk across the green to the iron railings and look down over the line of the city wall into the Longbrook valley; here you can see how the wall builders took advantage of natural features for the defence of the city. In Victorian times, catacombs were excavated into the hillside here. Look across to the Parish of St David's; the massive spire of St Michael's Church dwarfs the more distant early-twentieth-century tower of St David's.

Turn left and follow the wall round to its western angle, and the attractive eighteenth-century **Bartholomew Terrace (17)**. From here there is a good view over the Exe valley to the hills of Exwick beyond, now largely built upon. At the end of the terrace is The Old Chapel (1817), for many years a warehouse but now restored to use as a place of worship, and opposite lies the imaginative housing development of Beedles Terrace, just outside the line of the city wall.

Cross Fore Street to West Street, where several old houses back onto the wall; further down is the **West Gate (18)**, partly demolished in 1815 though one bastion still survives. Much history was made here: a rebel attack was repulsed in 1549, and Prince William of Orange made his first entry into an English city in 1688 after landing at Brixham. Stepcote Hill was then the main route into the city from the west, across the medieval Exe Bridge (twelfth century, and recently re-exposed, is visible from West Gate). **St Mary Steps Church (19)** has been here since about 1250, with its Matthew the Miller Clock dating from 1621 and restored in 1980. Close by are The House that Moved, a sixteenth-century timber-framed building moved to its present corner site from Frog Street in 1961, and simple fifteenth-century timber-framed houses in situ. Despite all the restorations this area more than any other captures the atmosphere of the medieval city.

The agile may dodge the traffic to cross Western Way (the inner bypass) and descend the steps to Cricklepit Street, which runs eastward just below the wall; it gives a view across the old industrial centre of the city, based on the leats (diversion channels from the main river) which drove the mills of the area. Walk along past Water Gate and a fragmentary water-wheel to the **Custom House (20)** (1688). The more prudent can walk instead up Western Way to the service station and use the underpass at Coombe Street; on the south side, walk past Tabernacle Court to the wall, look down over it where it is fallen away to see the water-wheel and Custom House, then descend Quay Hill to the quay.

The Port of Exeter centres on the quay, with the Custom House and Wharfinger's House close by; recent excavations have revealed that the modest building next to it (now an interpretation centre) was built on a sixteenth-century wharf, still complete with mooring rings. The cannon (1789) were taken as payment of port dues in 1819 and placed here in 1984 – they have never been fired in anger. Progressive development is aimed at enhancing the historic atmosphere of the area, and several newer buildings have been removed and older ones renovated. Note the two imposing warehouses (1835).

A ferry crosses the river at this point, leading to the nineteenth-century canal basin and connects the two parts of the **Maritime Museum (21)**. The Exeter Canal was built in 1563 and subsequently lengthened to provide a direct link with the sea; it is still navigable and has the oldest pound lock in the country.

Leave the quay by the steps beside **The Prospect Inn (22)** and walk up to Friar's Gate; among the interesting buildings of this area, notice Magnolia House on the site of the Friary. On the left, the city wall shows greatly varied stonework due to continual repair over the centuries, culminating in the disgraceful red brick insisted on by the Department of the Environment. A short detour eastward will take you to the gracious early-nineteenth-century houses of **Colleton Crescent (23)**. Cross at the traffic lights and proceed to **South Gate (24)**, where stones in a shrubbery mark the outline of a Roman bastion. Looking down South Street you can see George's Meeting, one of the finest Unitarian chapels in the country, now restored with some taste and in use as an up-market shopping centre.

From the South Gate, walk along the outside of the city wall across Trinity Green to **Southernhay (25)**; on your right is the former Royal Devon and Exeter Hospital (1742), one of the earliest provincial hospitals. Southernhay was a speculative development in the eighteenth and nineteenth centuries, when the city expanded beyond its walls, and is a good example of Georgian town planning. Its magnificent terraces, graced with Coade stone door-heads, are largely intact, with only minor

11

The Custom House, Exeter

modern development – some of which is harmonious – and the flower displays are well worth seeing in season.

From Southernhay, turn left into **Cathedral Close (26)** under the small iron bridge (1814). Although dominated by the **Cathedral (27)**, the attractiveness of this grassy precinct lies both in its variety of shops and houses and in its relative calmness away from the bustle of High Street. The cathedral was started in 1107, east of the site of a Saxon minster: recent archaeological evidence shows Christian burials since Roman times. There was also a Roman bath-house here. Major reconstruction of the Norman cathedral began in 1270, virtually completed in 1369, with minor additions since then including repair of bomb damage and the present restoration programme. We leave you to contemplate the massive Norman towers, the intricate window tracery, the famous image screen of the west front, and the sense of immense permanence. Think what it must have looked like in the thirteenth century, before the timber-framed houses were built – how it must have towered over all the lowly houses of the city!

Your walk has taken you through two thousand years of a city's existence: Exonians are proud to have as their motto *Semper fidelis* for they were always (well, nearly always) faithful to the Crown.

BUDLEIGH SALTERTON

Budleigh Salterton was once a part of the Manor of Budley Syon. Until 1894 it belonged to the parish of East Budleigh (see p.31). 'Salterton' means 'the settlement of salters'; salt-pans have been worked on the estuary perhaps since Roman times. Fear of pirates kept the coast sparsely populated.

As late as 1809, Salterton was a hamlet of only twenty-five houses. By 1830 it had begun to attract visitors due to 'the salubriousness of the air and the picturesque beauty of its scenery'. Soon it became a fashionable resort, with elegant residences, lodging-houses and many private day and boarding-schools. The gasworks appeared in 1867, the hospital in 1888 and the railway in 1897.

The earliest surviving buildings are mostly cob and thatch. The mid-nineteenth-century houses are often marked by round-headed windows, recesses and archways; others are taller with fretted barge-boards under gabled roofs.

Today it is a popular retirement area. Many of the former hotels, schools and lodging-houses have been replaced by flats or rest-homes.

Start from the free car park overlooking the **green (1)**. Pass the **public hall (2)**, cross Station Road and turn left at the public library by the brook. **St Peter's Church (3)** was built in 1893–4 by G. H. Fellowes-Prynne, and paid for by the Hon. Mark Rolle. The proposed tower on the north-west corner was never built. The church was severely damaged by a bomb in 1942.

The terrace of six timbered houses (twentieth century) in **The Lawn (4)** leads uphill to West Terrace; this corner is seen at its best in the spring when the trees are in bloom. Proceed towards Chapel Street; below the crossroads on the right is **Lyndale (5)**, an early-nineteenth-century house with lozenge-shaped windows and diamond and cross tracery.

At the west end of East Terrace, practically on the crossroads, the Chapel of Ease used to stand. This chapel, built by Lord Rolle in 1812 and enlarged in 1837, served the town until the consecration of St Peter's.

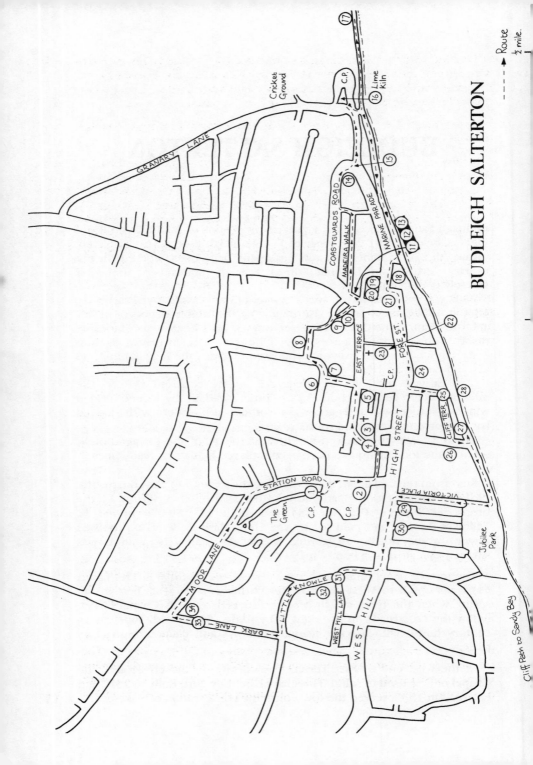

BUDLEIGH SALTERTON

- - - - - Route

½ mile.

Cliff Path to Sandy Bay

Turn up Chapel Hill, which is dominated by **Prospect House (6)**, with its central arched niche. On the right bend is **Ivy Bank (7)**, an L-shaped thatched cottage (late eighteenth century) with curved walls, probably because of carts scraping past the sharp bend.

Pause for a view of town from seat above Lantern House. On the horizon to your right is the East Devon Golf Course (1902).

Follow the cob wall uphill and turn down the lane on the right. The layering of the cob is clearly visible where the roughcast has worn away. Above on the left is **Watch Hill (8)**, one of Salterton's finest houses (late 1920s). The spinney on the right, colourful in the spring, belongs to **Umbrella Cottage (9)**; this L-shaped thatched house consists of a row of cottages to which a south-east wing was added in 1805. Note the porch. Turn right along the cul-de-sac for a better view of the intricately patterned windows and tented verandah.

Descend the steps to East Terrace. To the right are **five red-brick houses (10)** with brick dentilled cornices, three-storey bows, flights of steps, iron railings and semi-basements. These houses, believed to be the first in the town to be built of brick, date from the turn of the nineteenth century.

Note the group of three dwellings **(11)** on the east side of Fore Street Hill opposite; **Hillcroft**, **Prospect Cottage** (eighteenth century) and the bow-fronted **Pear Tree Cottage** (on the east side of Prospect Cottage).

The local name for Fore Street has, for over a century, been 'Surgery Hill'. **Little Hill (12)**, formerly Simcoe House, has been modernized and enlarged. It was once owned by General Graves Simcoe, who was in command of the Western District (1798–1806) when an invasion by Napoleon was believed imminent.

Lion House (13) is a mid-nineteenth-century Italianate stuccoed villa. There are fine iron railings and four piers, surmounted by pineapples and lions.

Turn right on Madeira Walk, overlooking the steep gardens of Marine Parade, and continue to Coastguards Road; here, turn right and cross. The late-nineteenth-century **Coastguards Cottages (14)** and small look-out (now demolished) replaced an original station on the Parade. The coastguards were Royal Navy men, and their longboat was rowed by a crew of eight.

From the **War Memorial (15)** look east to see the estuary of the Otter, the far bank fringed with pines, and terminating in Otterton Ledge. The estuary was made into a nature reserve in 1982; it is frequented by many varieties of sea birds. To the west is a panorama of town and beach, with the red sandstone cliffs (enclosing the famous Pebble Bed) rising to West

Down Beacon (425 feet high), beyond which lie Straight Point and the Exe estuary.

Turn down Saltings Hill. On the island between the two lanes by the car park are the remains of the once 20-feet tall **Lime Kilns (16)**; the bricked-in openings face the car park. The kilns were in use up to 1875. Limestone and coal used to be hauled up the shingle on rails.

The footpath on the **shingle ridge (17)** leads to the river mouth. There used to be a ferry. The heavy storms of the 1960s undermined this ridge; it has been reinforced by gabions (pebbles in wire cages).

Turn west on the coastal path. An exposed section of the sandstone has weathered into interesting shapes, and is overgrown by Hottentot Fig.

Before the first houses were built on Marine Parade in the early nineteenth century (rebuilt in this century), the whole area was an open field – the Water Ledge (or Leat) Field. The boats on the beach, now few in number, are a reminder of the extensive fishing of the past. As recently as 1939 there were bathing-machines. In the nineteenth century, ladies bathed at the eastern end, and gentlemen at the western.

Opposite the **Gentlemen's Club (18)** (early nineteenth century) is the **Octagon (19)** (built 1818), where Sir John Everett Millais made sketches for his famous painting 'The Boyhood of Raleigh' (1870).

Fairlynch (20) is a cottage orné (1811–2) with gothic windows and an octagonal thatched lantern. It was converted into a museum and arts centre in 1967; the extensions were built in 1977. One room is devoted to local history.

The seaward side of **Mackerel Square (21)** consists of four early-nineteenth-century houses including the Old Clink, formerly the police station. The square is overpowered by 'Walters' Folly', a tall brick building decorated by Italian craftsmen and erected by Mr Walters, the butcher, in 1889.

The brook runs along the roadway in Fore Street, with several small bridges. It used to run open across Mackerel Square before being bridged, and later culverted. Note the **'dipping steps' (22)** at the foot of Pebble Lane.

The **Temple Methodist Church (23)** was built in 1904–5, on the site of an earlier church (1811). The adjacent school room dates from 1884. Next to it is Abele Tree House (1804; rebuilt 1906). Three fine trees grow along the brook.

The **Rolle Flats (24)** were built in 1976/7 on the site of the Rolle Hotel, which was demolished in the early 1970s. The hotel was well established by 1830 and for over a century was the focal point of the town. The hotel's mews and stables used to be across Fore Street, where there is now a public car park.

Umbrella Cottage, Budleigh Salterton

The Fairlynch Museum

Turn left down Rolle Road, and take second right, **Cliff Terrace (25)** with its elegant (mostly nineteenth-century) houses and gardens extending to the cliff path. At the top, facing you, is **The Cliff (26)**, with an interesting ground-floor extension to the north decorated with stained-glass windows. This used to be the famous Library owned by Dr T. N. Brushfield (1828–1910), local historian. Thomas Adolphus Trollope (1810–1892), author of *History of Florence* and elder brother of Anthony, lived in 'Cliff Corner' (now demolished and replaced by Cliff House), on the corner of Cliff Terrace and Cliff Road.

Rejoin the coastal footpath, and descend a few yards to examine two interesting **gazebos (27)**; the rectangular one was used in the nineteenth century as a fishermen's chapel; below it is a round cob house with chimney and conical thatched roof.

From here there is a good view of the Terraces, Watch Hill (8) and Umbrella Cottage (9). Below are the **Steamer Steps** down to the beach **(28)**, so called because pleasure steamers picked up passengers from the beach here (1890–1934).

Walk uphill to the top of Victoria Place and on to level Jubilee Field for a view of the coastal panorama to Beer, and on clear days even to Portland Bill.

Descend Victoria Place, noting the nineteenth-century cottages on the left. Cross the road, turn left into Station Road, and so return to your starting-point.

Alternatively, turn left on West Hill. The first tall building is the **Masonic Hall** (1891) **(29)**. At the foot of Penlee once stood the **Public** or **Assembly Rooms (30)**, built in 1862 and bombed in 1942. They contained a good library; 350 persons could be seated for public dinners, functions, plays and concerts.

Most of Westbourne Terrace was built in the 1860s. Cross the road and turn right into **Little Knowle (31)**. Passing the Baptist or **Ebenezer Chapel** (1844) **(32)**, the oldest surviving church in Salterton, follow the S-bend towards an open field on the left and the crossroads; the road on the left fords the brook. Turn right up **Dark Lane (33)** – one of the oldest tracks in the district – an aptly named place with the roots of the overhanging trees emerging from the eroded sandstone banks.

At the top of Dark Lane is the **cemetery (34)**, with lich-gate, presented to the town in 1900 by the Hon. Mark Rolle. Turn right along Moor Lane back to The Green.

The chapters on Otterton, East Budleigh and Budleigh Salterton were contributed by the Otter Valley Association. The Association, which covers the five parishes up to Newton Poppleford, was formed in 1979, and currently has some 1000 members.

Dr Brushfield's library at 'The Cliff

Bibliography

Budleigh Salterton, Early Days Remembered: a Tribute to Maria Gibbons, Otter Valley Association (1987).

Budleigh Salterton in Bygone Days, Jim Gooding (Devon Books, 1987).

The Lower Otter Valley: Sketches on Local History, Otter Valley Association (1984).

Twelve Walks in the Otter Valley, Otter Valley Association (1982).

Otterton: A Devon Village, E. Michael Harrison (1984).

Devon Mill, Desna Greenhow (Charles Skilton, 1981).

Raleigh's Birthplace, by Lilian Sheppard (Granary Press, 1983).

'Otter Estuary' in *Devon Estuaries,* ed. Graham Wills (Devon Books, 1985).

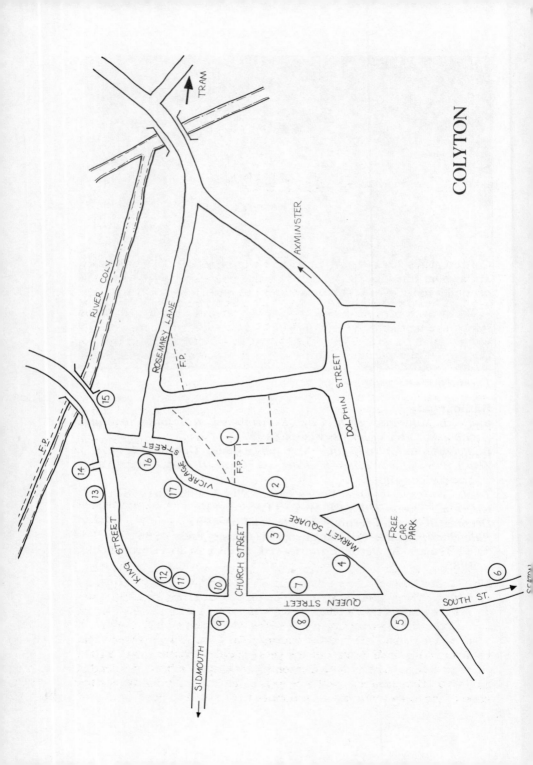

COLYTON

COLYTON

Colyton dates back to at least Saxon times and is rich in history. Throughout the ages Colyton has been a caring society and this continues today with a special welcome being given to new faces.

The **church of St Andrew (1)** is in the centre of the town and so we start our tour there. The building bears traces of many periods and a written guide is available in the church. The lantern tower with the lantern built on the square Norman tower is one of only three in the country (Ely Cathedral and Boston Stump in Lincolnshire are the others). There are interesting gargoyles and other stonework below this. The Saxon cross now in the south transept was found in pieces in the tower after a disastrous fire in 1933. It was removed and reassembled and is now recognized as one of the best-preserved Saxon crosses. The Pole monuments are to be found in the south aisle behind a beautiful stone screen built in the sixteenth century. The lovely west window with its stone tracery was glazed in 1902. An earlier west window is now preserved in the Beer Quarry Museum.

The market-place has many interesting buildings. The **Church House (2)** dates from 1546 and was the original meeting-place of the Feoffees and housed the grammar school until 1927. Note the stained-glass windows.

Opposite are the offices of an estate agent and a solicitor (3). Both have Tudor ceilings. The estate agent's has an interesting sixteenth-century archway, and a sixteenth-century mural has recently been revealed in the solicitor's office. The **town hall (4)** is in the centre of the town and is the home of Colyton Feoffees. The Chamber was founded in 1546 when Henry VIII had his cousin, John Courtenay, executed and confiscated his lands. Some Colyton yeomen collected the sum of £1000 – a fortune then – and rode to London to buy some of it back by a deed of feoffment. The chamber continues to use the revenue from this for the good of the town and it is a great honour to be asked to serve.

At the top of the town is a fountain (5), now a signpost; the inscription is well worth reading. Turn left to see **Great House (6)**, built in the sixteenth century of local flint. It was the home of the Yonge family and the Duke of Monmouth was entertained here.

Go back to the fountain and straight down Queen Street to **Coombe House (7)** on the right. This was a nonconformist vicarage until 1906 and services were held in the chapel behind which is now a YMCA and day centre.

Opposite is **Oroolong House (8)** owned by a Capt. Henry Wilson in the eighteenth century. He had been kidnapped and held on the island of Oroolong in the Pacific. He brought back Prince Lee Boo, the son of the King of the Islands but sadly he died of smallpox. The house is Georgian and only two rooms are on the same level.

Fifty yards further on, on the left, is **Colyton Cottage (9)**, built before 1600. It is built of stone and flint with cob behind rendered walls and has recently been beautifully rethatched. Over a fireplace in a bedroom is the text '"Who so feareth the Lord shal prospere and in the date of his end shal be blessed" 1610 EVMV'. Judge Jeffreys stayed here during the Bloody Assizes, which may account for a reputed ghost.

On the opposite corner is **Queenshaye (10)**, with a beautiful Georgian front. During renovation a deep well was found under the sitting-room floor. The back garden has a gazebo and an ice-house.

Beyond the garage is **Old Court House (11)**. It has an Adam staircase, fireplaces and doors. It is so called because it is believed that Judge Jeffreys held court here and there is a recent plaque commemorating the Colyton men who were put to death just outside. Next door is **Kingdon Cottage (12)**, which was probably joined with the next houses to form a Devon longhouse.

Continue down to the bottom of King Street to some fine Georgian houses (13) – Geleen, Althea and St Clements. Note the fire insurance protection plate on Althea. Turn left to the **tannery (14)**, where leather is still produced by the traditional oak bark method. Although modernized, parts are over 400 years old.

Further down King Street is the **Chantry** and **Chantry Bridge (15)**. This is probably the site of the old chantry fields let to provide an income for the priest.

Turn up Vicarage Street, past the 200-year-old Georgian **Colyton House (16)** with its high walls, and on the corner you will come to the fine vicarage and **Brerewood House (17)**. This is one of the town's oldest buildings, with fine Tudor carvings including the arms of Bishop
Veysey of Exeter (whose jewels are reputed to be buried in the house),

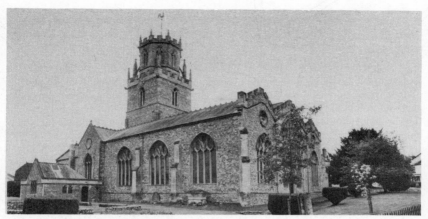

St Andrew's Church, Colyton

Colyton market-place

the Tudor rose and the Pomegranate of Catherine of Aragon, who is said to have stayed here after a shipwreck near by.

We have now come full circle back to St Andrew's Church but we have passed by many other interesting places, so if you have time come again and try out *Walk Around Colyton* produced by the primary school and the Walks leaflet produced by the Parish Council.

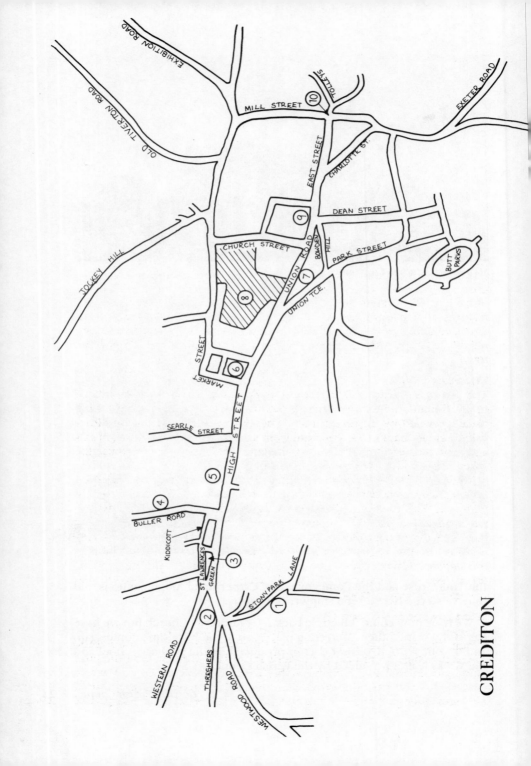

CREDITON

CREDITON

Stonypark and Tinpot Lane (1)
An old track now used as a short cut to and from Queen Elizabeth's Lower School (during fine weather). The high earth banks suggest its great age; it can usually be assumed that, in Devon, the deeper a lane, the older it is. This might be regarded as one of the main archaeological features of Crediton. The word 'park' comes from the Saxon *parc*, an enclosed field, which is another clue to the age of the lane. The first gate on the left-hand side going up provides a good point for viewing the town.

Landscore (2)
This is a very old street. The name is Anglo-Saxon and is probably related to the boundaries of the original Saxon town. Such boundaries were usually formed by digging a ditch. The earth was thrown up on either side to create banks to keep cattle from straying. Such a ditch, when raw and new, thus created a 'score' on the land. It was convenient to use the space between the two banks as a thoroughfare.

The Creedy Valley was one of the first areas of Devon to be colonized by the Saxons. Landscore, leading to Westwood Road, later became known as 'Ye Old Waye'. Threshers Road, which also leads off Landscore, was probably a farm lane connecting with the Copplestone road. The main way out of the town to the north ran over the high ground towards Sandford. In the 1830s Western Road was cut so that traffic could pass through the town centre. Just off Threshers Road, on the right going down, lies the ancient chapel of St Lawrence which now belongs to Queen Elizabeth's School.

Saint Lawrence's Green (3)
A large stone socket can be seen in the rosebed in the centre of the Green. This was originally the base of the town cross which stood at the top of the High Street near the baker's shop. This cross marked the limit of the market area. For many years the Green was a piece of fenced waste ground, and was restored for Queen Victoria's Diamond Jubilee. One of the remaining gate-posts stands next to the telephone box. On part of

25

this area stood a small building which was burnt down in 1743 and which stood on the site of a much earlier chantry. The feast of St Lawrence was marked by a fair lasting three days.

Opposite the Green is a building erected in 1860 to house Queen Elizabeth's Grammar School. A school existed in the Middle Ages, and after the closing of the monasteries by Henry VIII it was re-established as a Free Grammar School in the Lady Chapel of the parish church. In 1572 it was endowed by Queen Elizabeth I.

Buller Road (4)

This road, which runs from the end of Kiddicott, just behind the High Street, was named in honour of General Sir Redvers Buller. General Buller, who was lord of the manor of Crediton, was a hero of the Boer War. He won the V.C. for personal bravery. A footpath from the bottom end of Buller Road leads into the High Street. From this point you will get some impression of the grandeur of this main street. Some of the three-storey houses here were used in making serge, a strong woollen cloth in great demand during the Crimean War. 'As fine as Kirton spinning' became a byword of those times. Some of the old weaving sheds stood in the courtyards at the back of these houses. If you return to the New Cut, the old weaving sheds would have been where the garages stand.

High Street (5)

If you turn left just a few yards down the High Street you will find the Congregational Church. Near by, the High Street widens considerably. This is where the stone cross stood. At one time, the High Street was in two parts, known as 'Broad Street' and 'Narrow Street'. No. 52, High Street is a fine example of an eighteenth-century town house. You may have time to sketch it. On the corner of Searle Street, now housing Townsend's furniture shop, is Crediton Town Hall. This was built in 1853 and contained an Assembly Room and a public reading-room.

Still on the left-hand side, the next turning you come to is Market Street, on the corner of which is the Ship Hotel. At one time the Inland Revenue Office was housed here.

The New Market (6)

In 1836, James Wentworth Buller, Esquire, Lord of the Manor, gave a new market to the townsfolk of Crediton, in order to clear the main street for 'improvement'. This included the creation of a coaching route running through the town to connect with the recently built turnpike road to North Devon. The old coach road skirted Crediton, running up Mill Steet, turning left to Jockey Hill and thence to Forches Cross, and on to West Sandford, Morchard Bishop and Chulmleigh. Forches Cross was the site of the gallows where felons were hanged.

The New Market included a Market House with a court room above. Market day was Saturday but a monthly cattle market was held as well, and in April an annual great cattle fair, which was the largest in the West of England. Today a large part of the market is occupied by Devon Fire Service, but if you walk around the site you will see the three remaining corner-houses, one of the original gateways, and the beamed structure of the Open Market.

The Mid Devon District Council offices at the bottom of Market Street are in the old police station. This was built in 1847, and served Crediton for over 120 years, until the present police station was built in Churchill Drive, just off St Lawrence's Green. When the old building was converted into offices, one of the original cells, complete with heavy bolted door and peep-hole, was retained by the Council. It can be inspected on request.

Union Road and Union Terrace (7)
Walk to the top of North Street, turn left, and you are in Union Road. This was so called because when it was built in 1836 as part of Mr Buller's road improvement scheme it united East Town and West Town. Before the making of Union Road the old thoroughfare went by way of what is now called Union Terrace, which leads to Park Street and Bowden Hill. Notice the fanlight on the first black-and-white house. As you go over the hill you will notice the narrow road and the old cottages. Recent improvements have led to the demolition of many old properties in this area. A walk down steep Bowden Hill brings you to the magnificent Church of the Holy Cross, Crediton's parish church.

Newcombe's Meadow and St Boniface Statue (8)
From the bottom of Bowden Hill, turn left into Union Road. Behind the War Memorial turn right into the path that leads down to Newcombe's Meadow. Look for the statue of St Boniface. He was the apostle of Germany and was martyred in 755 A.D. St Boniface is the patron saint of Germany and Holland. A St Boniface festival is held in the town each August. This has really taken over from the three ancient fairs which the town once held.

The Church of the Holy Cross (9)
Return to the parish church by following the footpaths in Newcombe's Meadow to the exit in Church Street. The cobbled lane on the north side of the churchyard used to be 15 metres nearer the church, and was known as 'Cold Harbour'. Between the wall and the vicarage meadow were originally a sexton's house, workhouses, clink (lock-up) and infants' schoolroom. The land close to Vicarage Lane was the school playground and the rest gardens and the grammar school master's stable and yard. The original site housed a collegiate residence, founded in 1107 for eighteen canons, eighteen vicars, four singing boys and four lay clerks. An archway on the north-east corner of the church house is the only relic of an old gaol.

Holy Cross Church, Crediton

In this area a medieval guild known as the 'Kalendar Haye' held its meetings on the first day of the month (or *kalends*) to transact business concerning sickness and burial benefits. The day concluded with a social meal.

The raised stone cross at the south-east corner of the churchyard stands on the site of a row of cottages and the Ring of Bells public house, which were still standing in 1911. Opposite the Drama Centre and Hayward cottages stood an ancient stone cross which marked the eastern limits of the town. At this spot an uprising occurred on 1 May 1355, when there was said to be a river of blood flowing down the main street.

A walk to the bottom of East Street will bring you to a road on the opposite side of Mill Street called Tolleys. Somewhere in the vicinity is reputed to be the birthplace of Winfrith, who grew up to become St Boniface. This is thought to be the site of the first Saxon town or farm estate in the area. 'Town' comes from the Saxon '*ton*', a farmstead.

The Eastern Exit (10)
The original way out of the town to Exeter ran by way of East Street, Mill Street and Exeter Road. At this point the road was too narrow for vehicles, which had to continue along Mill Street to Jockey Hill and Forches Cross. At the bottom of Jockey Hill the former Horse and Jockey, which was once a busy inn, has been carefully converted into a very attractive thatched dwelling.

The road to Tiverton also ran along Mill Street and up what is now the Old Tiverton Road. The present main road, Exhibition Road, was made early in the twentieth century. Near the White Hart was the original Creedy Barton, the home farm of the Bishop until the nineteenth century. Rebels in the Western Prayer Book Rebellion assembled here in the summer of 1549 on their way to attack Exeter. They joined up with a force from Cornwall and barricaded the Exeter Road. This led to a fierce skirmish, well described in *Devon and its People* by Professor W.G. Hoskins (pages 79 to 84).

Park Road, leading to Park Street, branches off at this junction. Winswood House belonged to the Bishop of Crediton. This ran alongside the boundary of an early hunting park. Park Street, which still has a row of old thatched cottages, was at one time known as 'Spinning Path', as the cottagers sat in the roadway in fine weather spinning woollen thread. Near by is a modern road called Butt Parks which marks the spot where the townsfolk practised archery.

From the White Hart to East Street the main road now passes along Charlotte Street. This was cut at the time of the highway improvements in 1836, and was named after the wife of Mr Buller, the lord of the manor. The Buller monument is situated at the north-east corner of the churchyard.

Almost opposite the church stands Haywards School. The school moved here in 1860 with the help of the Hayward Charity which helped

29

Crediton High Street

educate and clothe 120 children. Their uniform was made of serge. Ernest Bevin, a famous former Foreign Secretary, was once a pupil at Haywards School. The present Youth Centre was the old boys' school. In the floor one can still see the row of brass studs where the pupils were aligned for monitorial instruction. Between the Youth Centre and the Drama Centre, which was the old girls' school, stand two houses where the headmaster and headmistress used to live.

Just beyond Hayward School, at the bottom of Bowden Hill, lies Dean Street, possibly the most ancient street in Crediton.

Kate Lowe,
Wembworthy Centre

EAST BUDLEIGH

East Budleigh stands in the Otter Valley at the head of what was once a wide estuary. It is an ancient village, becoming important enough to be a royal manor of a Saxon king, with an estimated area of 1500 acres of arable land by Domesday. The manor lay in the Hundred of Budleigh; during the Norman period, it was the largest hundred in Devon. In the twelfth and thirteenth centuries it was divided into five manors. The names of these are still used to designate areas of the parish: Higher Budleigh, Lower Budleigh, Hayes, Tidwell and Dalditch. By 1832 all five manors had finally come into the possession of the Rolle Estate (now the Clinton Devon Estates).

The early development and prosperity depended on agriculture, wool production, and trade through the port of Budley Haven, situated on the west bank of the River Otter south-east of the village. The port was used extensively until the mid-fifteenth century, when a shingle spit gradually barred the entrance to all but shallow-draught vessels.

The present village is a mixture of old and new: cob-and-thatch cottages of the seventeenth and eighteenth centuries, some added in the nineteenth century, and, more recently, extensive areas of modern housing to accommodate mostly retired residents.

From the free car park pass into Church Lane up the steps to the churchyard and the south porch. **All Saints' Church (1)**, built of local sandstone, stands in a commanding position above the village. The first recorded vicar served the church in the mid-thirteenth century, when it was a simple building with a low tower, a nave and a single aisle and a small chancel. There were extensive additions to the church in the fifteenth century: the present tower is 20 feet square at the base, and rises 80 feet to the top of the embattled turret. Two yew trees to the west of the porch may have been planted in the late seventeenth century. From the porch of the church there is a good view of the central part of the parish. Visit the church: inside an illustrated guide is available, giving details of the famous carved bench-ends, and the historic connections with Sir Walter Raleigh (or Ralegh, as some scholars prefer).

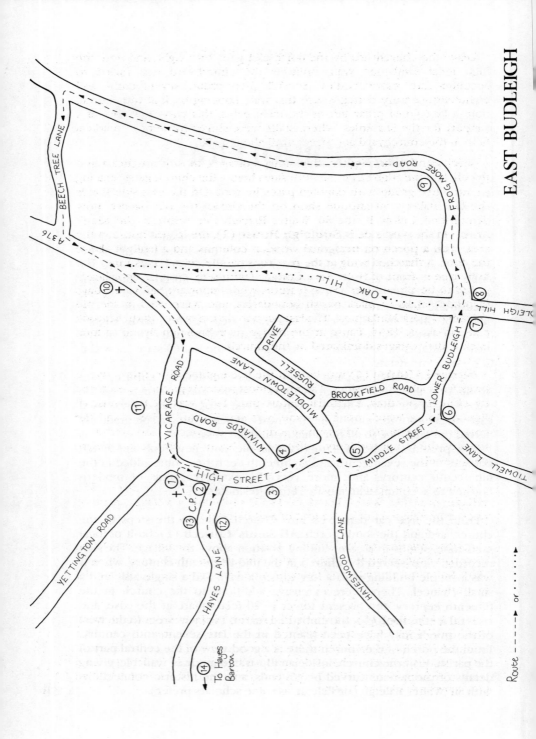

EAST BUDLEIGH

Route ------ or ....

Leave the churchyard by the north-east gate, turn right, and note the high local sandstone wall, built as the churchyard was raised to accommodate more bodies. Several picturesque seventeenth- and eighteenth-century cottages face this wall. Looking back at the church, note a hexagonal pillar left of the main gates; this was once part of a support for the Shambles, where stalls were stored for Sunday markets held in the churchyard and street until about 1600.

Seventeenth- and eighteenth-century cottages, mostly roughcast and thatch, line the High Street on both sides below the church gates, making an attractive group with cobbled paths in front. On the east side stands the Old Bakery, an antique shop on the site of the old bakery, now demolished; below it, the Sir Walter Raleigh Inn, formerly the King's Arms. On the west side is **Budleigh House (2)**, the largest house in the area, with a porch on octagonal wooden columns and a fanlight above the door. A thatched wing at the rear runs parallel with Hayes Lane. The holly tree in front of Holly Tree Cottage (with semi-circular door-head) is said to be a 'mark-tree'. Such features were important before the days of proper maps to mark parish boundaries, and were used in the old custom of 'perambulations'. The last perambulation of East Budleigh took place in about 1854. Pause at the bridge over Budleigh Brook to look back at the cottages dominated by the church.

Wynard's House (3) was built in the late eighteenth century, with a brick front and stucco sides. The uppermost storey is pierced at each end by a lunette window. A familiar feature until 1977 was the toll-house or Round House which used to stand between Wynard's House and the cottages to the north. A hexagonal structure built of cob, and narrowing towards the top, it suddenly collapsed. All that now remains is a plaque on the wall.

Budleigh Brook runs down the left-hand side of Middle Street. The **village hall (4)** was erected in 1955, replacing a village 'institute' housed in a Nissen hut at the foot of Middletown Lane.

At the junction of Middletown Lane stands a memorial to Queen Victoria's Golden Jubilee (1887), when the combined efforts of the Hon. Mark Rolle and the villagers brought piped water to the village for the first time.

Drake's School (5) was built in 1860 to replace an earlier school. The name commemorates Robert Drake's charitable bequest to East Budleigh. A row of ornamental brick cottages bearing the initials M.R. (Mark Rolle) and the dates 1874 and 1875 stand on the left. Disused steep steps opposite these cottages lead to the site of the first Budleigh School (1847–1860).

East Budleigh High Street seen from the churchyard

34   *Thatched cottages and Budleigh Brook in Middle Street*

A group of seven large horse-chestnut trees (6) mark the site of the pound, where stray animals were impounded. Some of the trees may be a century old.

Budleigh Brook reappears on the left-hand side of Lower Budleigh, with several attractive little bridges. Early-nineteenth-century cottages, mostly roughcast over cob, with thatched, pantile or slate roofs, stand on both sides of the road. Diamond Cottage has a trellis porch and patterned panes. Some flint walls and a garden running down to the brook add to the attractiveness of the area.

The road widens as you approach the crossroads. The **Rolle Arms Inn** (7) was built in 1756, probably replacing an earlier hostelry on the same site. Originally the Exeter Inn, it was renamed in 1820.

On the south-east corner stands **Christopher's (8)**, a sixteenth-century cottage named after the first village doctor, William Christopher. Formerly it housed a tannery which supplied leather buckets for the Tudor navies. The disused chapel to the east, the Gospel Hall, was built partly at the doctor's expense. Once a poor-house also stood on the crossroads.

Now either follow the main road (the A376) north for a third of a mile, or take the longer alternative (almost a mile) to avoid traffic, by turning east along Frogmore Road. You will pass **Thornmill Farm (9)** on the site of the lowest of the three mills which drew water from Budleigh Brook; it served the manor of Lower Budleigh. As the road winds north you can see over the hedge on your right the distant trees on the bank of the Otter. The land between was marshes, so all the cottages are on the left-hand side, and each cottage stands end-on to the road with any outbuildings at the rear. Turn left along Beech Tree Lane, and left again on the A376.

The two suggested routes meet at the fork, where stands the **Salem Chapel (10)**, the original Dissenters' Chapel. Built in 1719, it was enlarged in 1837 and restored in the 1970s.

Return to the churchyard along Vicarage Road, passing the **vicarage (11)** (1856) on your right. An ancient inn, The Five Bells, was demolished to make room for the vicarage drive.

Recross the churchyard and from the south-west gate look south-west over the car park at **Vicar's Mead (12)**. This L-shaped thatched house was the vicarage in which Walter Raleigh reputedly had lessons in his youth. There is a fine thatched cob wall running parallel to the road. The house has tunnels within and below it for the convenience of former vicars who did a good 'trade' in smuggling spirits. The gardens are open to the public on a few Sundays each year.

On the site of the car park stood the tithe barn, where wheat, barley, etc. collected as taxes was stored, and where churchwardens brewed ale for Ale Feasts. One of the three parish forges stood across Hayes Lane, where the galvanized lorry garage is now. To the west of the car park note **Hill Farm (13)** and the adjoining seventeenth- and eighteenth-century cottages. Up the lane behind these cottages, towards the new church hall, stood the Town Mill, serving Higher Budleigh. Pulled down some fifty years ago, it is a place of pilgrimage for Americans, as Roger Conant was born there in 1592. He sailed for America in 1623, and founded the Massachusetts Bay Colony in Salem three years after the arrival of the Pilgrim Fathers.

To reach **Hayes Barton (14)**, the birthplace of Sir Walter Raleigh, follow Hayes Lane for about one mile. This is a fine medieval cob-and-thatch house, repeatedly restored and still occupied. The main rebuilding was probably in Elizabethan days, when the addition of two wings to the south and a Devon porch between created an E-plan, possibly as a compliment to the Queen. Various relics of Raleigh are kept in the room where he is said to have been born.

Otter Valley Association
(See p.18)

EXMOUTH

Walk 1: The Parade, Manchester House, the Docks and the Front

Exmouth is a town well worth looking at with care. Its history goes back more than a thousand years, and with a discerning eye much of the past can be reconstructed. Let us start our first walk at the busy corner where the upper Parade turns north to become Exeter Road. Here lies what was once the heart of the place. The Exe and its marshes came up to this point and covered all one can see to the west and south-west. From here, at **Mona Island (1)** (now the paved area outside Glenorchy Hall) the ferry sailed to the other side of the river, owned and used by the monks of Sherborne, who owned much of the land on both sides of the Exe. From this point we can see along Chapel Street (the Magnolia Centre) which was once the waterfront and where medieval foundations have been excavated. In this street stood St Margaret's Chapel, now pulled down, but its holy-water stoop is preserved in St Anne's Roman Catholic church at Brixington. The site is marked on the wall by a plaque.

We will now walk along the raised pavement towards the town and can see on our right, behind the modern shop façades, a few fine houses, once the most desirable residences in the town and similar to those built on the Beacon. They were built on an embankment against the river, and the marsh behind them was drained some years later with another embankment which enclosed 40 acres of land, and began in earnest the reclamation of tidal land on which the town now stands.

On the left of the raised pavement on the other side of the road much has been swept away by development, including the medieval street plan and a charming row of small Georgian cottages with tiny front gardens, a feature which could well have delighted many more generations. All that remains is the original stone name-plaque, Staples Buildings 1810, on the end gable of the new development, and you'll have a difficult job to spot that.

We then reach the rest of the Parade, now at street level, and pass a broad open circus **(2)** in the centre of which now stands the mini-roundabout and formerly stood the 'Great Tree' which marked the   37

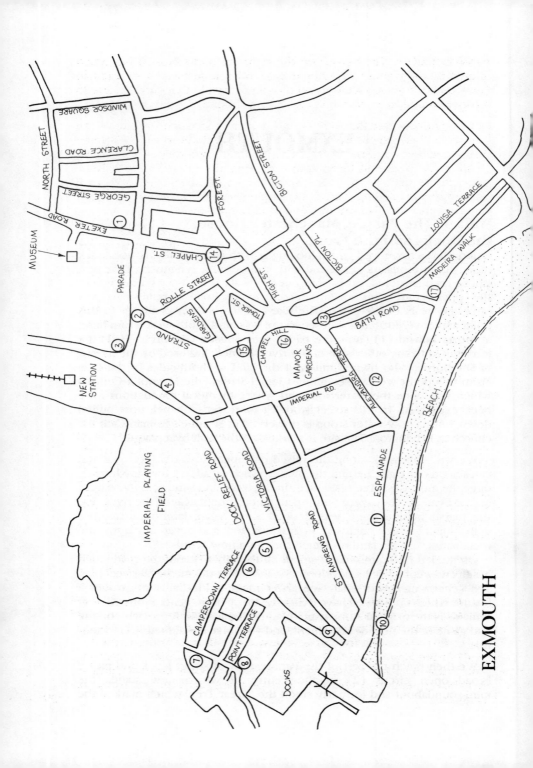

EXMOUTH

parish boundary. The houses on the right are mid-Victorian but much altered by the present day shop-fronts, and behind these is a large hall (now used for bingo) standing on the site of the old Exmouth Theatre in which Edmund Kean gave readings from Milton on several occasions.

We continue past the subway and gardens (3), once the site of the railway station, which was first used in 1861, rebuilt in the 1920s and finally demolished in the 1980s, when the railway terminus was moved to allow the ring road through to the town. The future of the railway, once threatened by the Beeching Axe, now seems assured, with improvements pending. The façade of the South Western Hotel is an apt reminder that the platform once stood only yards away.

The swimming-pool, sports centre and Imperial playing fields are on more reclaimed land, and roughly on the site of the sports centre formerly stood a wooden jetty on to which cargoes of incoming ships were landed from lighters which trans-shipped to larger vessels anchored in the river.

On our left is **Manchester House** (4), a Georgian building constructed of mellow red brick, now lamentably covered with a dreary wash, in which the notorious Mary Ann Clarke lived in 1804. She was the mistress of the Duke of York, brother of the Prince Regent, and ran a splendid racket selling appointments in the government and army in which the Duke was implicated. There was a scandal, and she bore the brunt of it, being sent to prison and dying in poverty and disgrace in Paris in about 1813. However, while in Exmouth she lived in tremendous luxury on her £12000 a year, handsomely supplemented by her patronage of positions. One can imagine the simple inhabitants of Exmouth gaping at her carriage, her clothes and her liveried servants. The rear elevation of Manchester House is well worth a diversion. The York Hotel a few yards away was formerly known as the Great Tree Inn and was a quaint thatched house until the end of the last century. After a suitable period had elapsed it changed its name to the York Hotel because of the local connection. The late Victorian rebuilding was very attractively done in a variety of brick.

Now we move along Imperial Road, which was formerly the waterfront, with a row of thatched cottages and a quay stacked high with barrels, bales and all manner of goods including coal. We join the line of the new relief road at the roundabout, emerging in Camperdown Terrace, and immediately facing us is the original **Sailors' Rest** (5) with its brickwork crest. On this site the venture was not successful, it being said to be *too* close to the docks, so it was rebuilt in St Andrews Road in 1907. In the First World War part of it was used as an officers' hospital, pioneering electrical treatment. The building in Camperdown Terrace, then being used as a children's seaside home, rang to the sound of laughter.

Exmouth docks

On the quay at Exmouth

To the left Camperdown Terrace meets Victoria Road. This junction commemorates the disastrous collision in the Mediterranean in 1893 between H.M.S. *Camperdown* and H.M.S. *Victoria* which resulted in the loss of the latter and 321 sailors. We, however, move westward along Camperdown Terrace and will soon see on the left a large three-storey building (6). The date 1810 is cut into the wall and it is one of the oldest buildings on the Point (as this area was known). It is still in use today as a sail-loft, its original function. In close proximity stood the windmill which we must picture situated in the midst of the sand-dunes that comprised the whole area. It disappeared about 1830. It had not been used for many years because during one particular storm the sails had revolved so fast that the works ignited with the friction, and it caught fire. Right at the end of Camperdown Terrace we see in front of us the **Trinity House buoy store** (7), which has been used in that connection since the river was buoyed in 1816. Further along, the rear garden wall of the houses in Point Terrace, constructed of white limestone, may be seen (8). This wall stretched back towards the sail-loft for a distance of over 200 yards and had a lean-to roof built up to it. Once this was a busy scene, with men turning the wheels that twisted hemp into the finest and strongest of ropes. These were required in huge quantities for shipbuilding, a trade that was also carried on here on a large scale amid the sand-dunes of the Point.

If you turn and look past the front of the buoy store there is a narrow ramp-way to the sea-shore. There in the inlet behind Camperdown Terrace were built sizeable sailing ships up until the 1880s, when steam and steel took over. Almost opposite the end of the rope walk on the opposite side of Shelly Road you may, if you look carefully, see some curved brickwork in the pathway to the chalets which looks like the top of a well. It is in fact the remains of the tar pit in which the pitch was boiled up for caulking. Not so long ago we would have been walking over dunes beside tidal creeks, all now built over, until we reached a rather larger creek than most known as Shell Pit or Lobster Hole. This natural inlet was in 1860 made into the docks and its sides walled with stone.

At the period the docks were built hundreds of ships came up the Exe from all over the world and lay at anchor in the Bight, a sheltered haven behind the Warren, before going on the tide to Topsham or Exeter via the canal. From that time Exmouth became a much busier port itself, its imports being much more easily landed directly from the ships, instead of via the lighters at the rather inaccessible jetty we talked of earlier. Now the multitude of sailing ships have gone (sometimes there were 100 or more at anchor in the Bight), but Exmouth is still a very busy port, with ships from all over Europe carrying timber, grain, potatoes, animal feed and a host of other commodities in and out of the dock at almost every tide. Until recently a flotilla of small pleasure- and fishing-boats could be seen, but commerce has ousted them to moorings in the river. Ironically, they may all be back, as there are plans to turn the dock into a marina. The boat-houses, (now summer-houses), some of which are nearly 100 years old, are also possible subjects for redevelopment.

The Starcross ferry leaves several times a day in the summer months from the dock entrance. In Henry VIII's time the ferry at Mona Island had passed from the monks to the Exeter Corporation and in 1844 it was purchased by the new South Devon Railway built by Brunel on the other side of the river mouth. There are connections with the main-line service.

From the docks we move to the sea front, passing on the left the **Beach Hotel (9)**, whose Lifeboat Bar houses a fine collection of photographs and equipment connected with the lifeboat, and is naturally the haunt of the seafaring fraternity. On the opposite side of the road is the Dock Company Office, a handsome, though rather neglected, building, also a potential subject for development. A little further on we come across the oldest part of the sea wall **(10)**, constructed in 1842, an excellent piece of engineering attributed to Smeaton's plans. If we look over the wall we can see the curve of the defences built in to minimize the power of the waves, and the massive stones which must have presented a monumental task to the masons endeavouring to position them in the days before mechanical assistance. Even today the defences cannot contain the severest of storms and water can cascade over the top. Further along, the wall was constructed on a different principle without a parapet but so much sand and water came over the road that one was added. It made little difference as the sea and sand continually battle to resume the position denied them since 1842.

On the left near the westward end of Morton Crescent stood a circular castellated house, never occupied, and nicknamed Cat's Castle. When Lady Nelson, who lived on the Beacon, had the bodies of her son, Josiah Nesbit, and his children transported from France for reburial, they were landed at Temple Steps too late to be taken to Littleham churchyard that night. The coffins were placed in the empty house for the night, and it was thereafter known as Corpse Castle and reputedly haunted. That fine terrace known as **Morton Crescent (11)** is a good example of late-Victorian symmetry. Originally built mainly as private residences the crescent now contains many flats and some of the town's finest hotels.

We now return to the town by Alexandra Terrace, noticing the Golden Jubilee drinking-fountain rediscovered after disappearing for twenty years and positioned by the museum in 1987, and passing on our right the Imperial Hotel, built in 1869 but much altered and rebuilt after a terrible fire in 1973. You cannot fail to notice its interesting early-nineteenth century copy of the Greek Temple of Theseus **(12)**, which has also unfortunately been much altered. Until the building of the hotel there stood a companion, the Temple of the Winds, but this was demolished to provide better access.

Under the cliff of the Plantation the old mill-wheel from Withycombe Village (13) is surrounded by a pretty little garden. If you look at the stone retaining wall of the hill behind the wheel you will notice some rectangular holes. These date from the time when the sea and sand-dunes infiltrated to this point. The fishermen would insert wooden poles into the wall and hang out the nets to dry and be repaired. The railings above have impaled at least one unfortunate horseman whose mount took fright whilst descending the hill.

So to the top of Chapel Hill, which we visit on another walk; from here we descend via Tower Street, beside the Pilot Inn. One of the medieval streets, still cobbled into this century, it was so named not because of the Methodist Church at the bottom but because, on looking up the street in former days you could see the tower of the Chapel of the Holy Trinity standing at the top. In ancient days Tower Street had a maze of little courts and alleys, each a little community of its own.

Crossing Rolle Street we enter the newly built pedestrian precinct over the area formerly the heart of Exmouth known as **The Cross (14)**; most of the area was destroyed by enemy action in the last war and the present redevelopment has resulted. A few steps along Chapel Street and we are back at the starting-point.

Walk 2: Gardens and Other Places of Interest

We start from the open space at the end of the Parade (2), where (as was mentioned in Walk 1) the Great Tree formerly stood. It was several hundred years old when felled in the late nineteenth century but as only one photograph survives its species is uncertain, though opinion leans towards its being a wych-elm. Crossing to the Strand Gardens we find that with a few exceptions the trees are those traditionally to be found in parks and gardens, many having been planted at the end of the last century. The word strand literally means 'place by the water', and (as we learned in Walk 1) before the land reclamation of the nineteenth century the estuary bounded the north-west side. Another name for the area was The Square. It was encroached upon at the southern end in 1832 by the building of the Market House whilst the northern half was grazing, garden and a bowling green for the Globe Hotel, which had been the principal coaching inn since the seventeenth century. When Rolle Street was cut through the maze of courts and alleys in 1866 the Globe had to go and Woodley's shoe-shop now occupies the site. At the same time the Strand Gardens were, in part, donated to the public and the remainder followed when the Market House was moved to another part of the town. Three corners are marked by fine horse-chestnut trees, at least one being indicated at the time of the Tithe map in 1844, whilst limes occupy the pavements on the western side. Plane trees also appear on the pavements and the conifers are represented by the yew on the east and Scots pine on the west sides. Palms are easily grown in the mild climate and are found within the gardens.

In the forecourt of Lloyds Bank will be seen a fine specimen of Exmouth magnolia, a species which was introduced from America through a local resident, Sir John Colleton, in the seventeenth century.

The ornate red-brick building fronting Rolle Street is the original town hall constructed in 1888, and at the opposite end of the gardens you will notice a small alleyway beside the newsagent's. This formerly led to Strand Court and the fish quays.

Leaving the Strand by the south-west corner we pass on our left a nice Regency terrace, altered at ground-floor level by shop-fronts, at the far end of which, next to the hairdresser's, remains part of Queen's Court.

On the right is an impressive building known as **West End House (15)**, and now the premises of Thomas Tuckers'. It was built in the late-eighteenth century as a residence for the mother-in-law of the owner of the Manor House, which stood in the Manor Grounds we shall visit shortly. In 1801, West End House, which literally was the western extremity of development, was purchased by a tradesman – Richard Webber – much to the horror of the gentry, and he quickly established the business which continues to flourish today in a refreshingly unchanged and unhurried way.

The large limestone building opposite, formerly a private house, is now part of the council offices; on leaving this to our right we enter the Manor Grounds. These were formerly the gardens of **Manor House (16)** (a rather pretentious name, considering it had no claim as such, but nevertheless it was a fine house). It stood on the site of the present toilets and behind these can still be seen the wine cellar reaching back under the roadway and now in use as an electricity sub-station. When the house was demolished in 1896, the gardens were acquired for public use.

Lime trees will be noticed in profusion, the usual lopping and pollarding having taken place to maintain reasonable size. One, near the council offices, has, however, escaped this treatment and flourishes.

Magnificent wych-elms dominated the gardens but unfortunately they shared the fate of all other elms in the 1980s. They stood close to the Turkey oaks. Adjacent to the car park you will notice the holm-oak with its evergreen holly-like leaf and also the fan-shaped leaves of the ginko tree. Still in the same area, on the lawns to the left of the perimeter paths is a Spanish or Lucombe oak, a hybrid variety introduced at Exeter in 1762. Mr Lucombe, who was responsible for this variety, was buried at the ripe old age of 103 in a coffin made from one of the seedlings of his original propagation. The monkey puzzle tree needs no introduction. Walk around the gardens at your leisure but as you make your way to the exit point in the south-east corner notice a rather untidy Midland hawthorn sprawled amid the bushes near the Information Bureau.

Between the Information Bureau and the central path you will notice two newly planted trees, one of which is a sycamore presented by the Exmouth Society. We cross now to the Plantation, Undercliffe or Madeira Walk as it is severally called, beside the water-wheel (13), mentioned in Walk 1, and immediately notice the sandstone retaining wall to the Beacon. Between some of the stones are open rectangular holes; fishermen used to put poles in these to hang their nets on. In the eighteenth century the sea flowed as far as the red sandstone cliffs as you will see a few paces on. A plaque commemorates the flood-lighting installed along the Walk in Jubilee year.

The Plantation had its origins in 1824 when the two Temples mentioned in Walk 1 were built amid the sand-dunes and some landscaping commenced. In 1838, Lord Rolle laid out the walkways we see today and commenced planting on a large scale. Until this century one of his liveried keepers would sound a horn at dusk and then close the gates for the night.

Taking the left-hand path that rises toward the Beacon we pass lopped beeches and a number of holly-like bushes which are in fact the stumps of holm-oaks planted for their resistance to the salty sea winds. Nearing the top of this path you will notice two large holm-oaks, about 170 years old, one of which is due to be felled. At this point take the path to the right and begin the descent, keeping an eye open for Turkey oaks with their long saw-like leaves; these were brought to this country in 1735. A few of the native Scots pines will be easily recognized by their tall trunks and 'crocodile skin'. Regaining the lower path we can see sycamore roots exposed on the left-hand bank whilst the Pavilion gardens on the right contain many palms and flowering cherries.

Reaching the junction with Carlton Hill we turn right to return along the Esplanade but the Plantation Walk continues straight on for another mile. More palms are to be seen as we return along the front, the sunken gardens being the Tennis Club's original courts. At first glance the **Deer Leap (17)** would not conjure thoughts of an historic building but beneath the twentieth-century façade lies one of the oldest buildings in the town – the Bath House. Here it was that in the 1790s two local doctors established their hot and cold, salt, fresh or mineral bathing facilities for the nobility and others who flocked to Exmouth to be cured of every manner of ailment. Surprisingly, the business lasted into the early 1900s, and during excavations of recent years the pipework running to the sea was uncovered. Here we turn into Bath Road, passing

The Strand Gardens, Exmouth

the rear of Elizabeth Hall (formerly the Gentlemen's Club) and seeing again the variety of now familiar trees before returning to the town.

Exmouth Museum

These two walks were originally published in 1978 by the Exmouth Society in a booklet entitled *Exploring Exmouth*. The Society continues to play an important part in preserving the character of old Exmouth.

HONITON

Although Honiton existed in Saxon times, the present town was laid out as a new town astride the old Roman highway in about 1200. It was set out on a regular grid pattern with the High Street running through the middle and with long narrow plots, all of equal lengths, marked out at right angles to it. There is still much evidence of this plan to be seen as you follow this trail.

Start in the High Street, at the **museum (1)**, the town's oldest building (a pamphlet on its history is available inside) and turn westwards. On the right is St Paul's Church, which dates from 1835. Inside you may see an interesting memorial to the Revd R. Lewis.

Beyond this is the **Angel (2)**. In the days of road travel by horse Honiton lay at a convenient distance from Exeter for a stop and the Angel is one of the many inns surviving from the coaching era. Others include the Dolphin, the Three Tuns and the Volunteer, whilst others, now shops, can be recognized by having an archway which led to the long stable-yard. The Black Lion has now disappeared completely but Black Lion Court, an imaginative new development opposite the Dolphin, perpetuates the name.

Just past the Dolphin is the **Pannier Market (3)**, now a shopping arcade but originally a market hall in which goods that had been brought into town in panniers slung on pack-horses were sold.

Continuing along the High Street, past the Three Tuns, **Central Place (4)** may be seen. This is one of several similar developments of worker's cottages built at right angles to the street along the length of one of the medieval new town plots. Others which may be looked for include King's Terrace, St John's Close and East View Cottages. Honiton was an important centre of the Devon cloth trade and these features are probably associated with that period.

On reaching the brow of the hill the remains of the River Crystal may be seen in the pavement on the south side of the street. This stream used to run the length of the High Street in an iron trough with dipping tanks

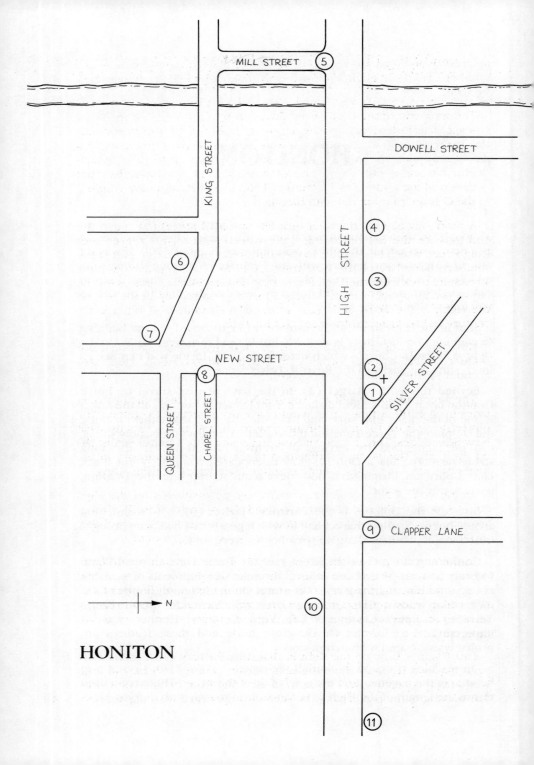

at intervals and thus was an important source of fresh water. In this area a number of pleasant eighteenth and early-nineteenth century houses may be seen.

The west end of the High Street descends into the valley of the River Giseage. This little river has been important in Honiton's history, for with the harnessing of water power it was used to drive mills. It is also associated with the town's disreputable election history, in which deplorable scenes of bribery and violence occurred. The fighting on the occasion of the Cyder Tax Election of 1763 is reported to have resulted in the Giseage running red with blood.

A short way beyond the river turn left into **Mill Street (5)** and at the end look for the last remaining water-wheel. Now turn left again into King Street, which lies parallel to the High Street and is, in fact, part of the southern boundary of the new town of 1200. The long narrow plots stretching back from the High Street may be seen in many places on the left as you go uphill from the Giseage. Just beyond the top of the hill, on the right, is the **Drill Hall (6)**, an excellent example of nineteenth-century Indian Army cantonment architecture!

King Street ends at a crossroads by the **Star Inn (7)**. Straight opposite is Queen Street; this was formerly the coach road to London, which may account for the inn being at this point.

The street running north and south is New Street. This name probably dates from 1200. A new street would have been needed to connect the old settlement on the hill with the new town, and this is exactly what New Street does. Turn left down New Street and note **Chapel Street (8)** on the right. This is the continuation of the southern boundary of the medieval new town and is in line with the main length of King Street.

At the end of New Street turn right and go eastwards up the High Street. Opposite the end of New Street and also opposite St Paul's church are excellent examples of first-floor cast-iron balconies, probably produced in the town by the now defunct Mickleburgh foundry.

In the eastern part of the High Street is much excellent eighteenth-century townscape on both sides of the street. In particular Nos. 79 and 81 retain their contemporary shop-fronts. On the left note **Clapper Lane (9)**, which leads to Clapper Bridge over the River Otter, most probably once of clapper construction. The old cast-iron signpost is worth inspecting.

Past Clapper Lane on the right is **Honiton Pottery (10)**. Pottery has been made in Honiton since the seventeenth century at least and until well into this century was made from clay dug from behind the works. The making of the pottery may be seen during normal working hours.

At the end of the High Street, on the left, is **Marwood House (11)** (*not* open to the public), which was built in 1619 by John Marwood, the second son of Thomas Marwood, physician to Elizabeth I. Marwood House has another connection with royalty, since it was here that Charles I slept on the nights of 25 July and 23 September during his Civil War campaign in the West.

John Yallop

Honiton High Street

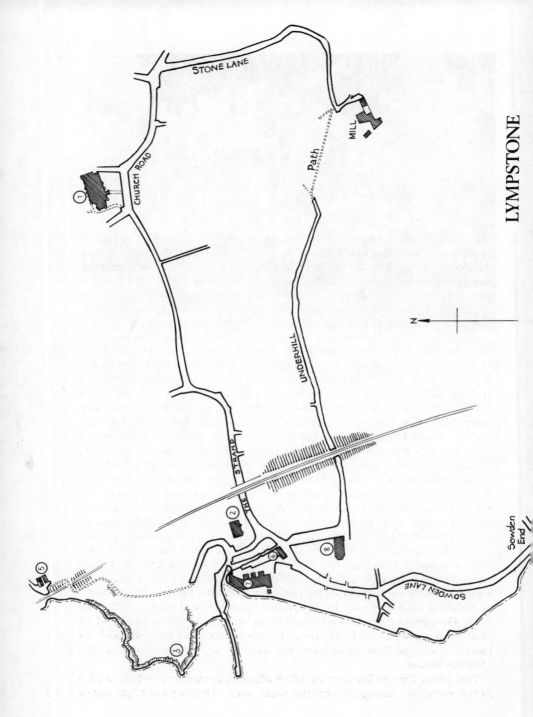

LYMPSTONE

LYMPSTONE

The village of Lympstone is snugly situated between two red promontories on the east bank of the River Exe, facing the parklands of the home of the Earls of Devon, Powderham Castle. It has had links with much of England's history for more than a thousand years. The name is thought to be derived from a name of Saxon origin, and appears in Domesday Book as Leustona, having been variously spelt down the ages. The present usage dates from about 1726.

Romans, Vikings, Saxons and Normans have all found their way up the Exe, and left their traces along the estuary. The recent Re-Survey of Devon points to a sizable Saxon settlement along the north side of the Watton Brook, a fishing community near the present Boat Shelter and a farming village further up, with the church, Town Farm and Mill, with Maltings attached, still working till just after the Second World War. The pattern of these early dwellings is still discernible. The earlier harbour was sited just beyond Parsonage Stile, where at one time there was a tryworks, processing whale blubber. The coming of the railway (c.1860) altered this, as it temporarily altered the use of the houses in the heart of the village (the soot drove the wealthier residents away and the properties became commercial). They remained however up Burgmann's Hill and towards the 'new road' constructed to take the general public away from the old road, which had followed the estuary along, virtually under the windows of Nutwell Court. These new houses were the homes of Exeter merchants seeking more salubrious surroundings, as Harefield, built for the Gattey family, and later the Peters (now St Peter's Preparatory School) and others built by speculators, seeking to charm the visitors barred from war-torn Europe. Many forms of building materials may be observed, from cob and thatch to locally made Georgian bricks, or Victorian bricks brought by the railway and, of course, the distinctive local stone. Dutch bricks, too, brought back as ballast from the Low Countries, are also to be seen in some of the chimney-stacks.

The Great Devon Mystery of 1855 affected Lympstone, when after a heavy snowfall, strange footprints were seen. This mystery has never really been explained and still causes speculation; some people firmly believed the footprints were those of the Devil himself.

Eden Phillpotts based one of his novels, *Redcliff*, on Lympstone, and his widow lived here.

The **Parish Church** of the Nativity of the Blessed Virgin Mary (**1**), a dedication unique in this country today, was largely restored in the nineteenth century, though the tower, chancel arch and north arcading date from 1409, when an earlier church was rebuilt. The Saxon font can be seen inside, left of the door.

Lympstone did not escape the Civil War. At different times, both sides fired across the estuary, trying to prevent supplies reaching Exeter. It is said they 'sighted' from the church tower, with guns on **Cliff Field** (**3**); this is now in the care of the National Trust and commands a wide view across the river. A path leads to it from behind the **Swan Inn** (**2**).

Beyond the Boat Shelter stands the **Darling Rock** (**4**), a shrunken remainder of its former glory, when it was so large, a cockle cart could barely drive between it and the cliff. Once part of the Rectorial Manor of Lympstone and only just beyond the confines of the Parish of Kenton, it is recorded in Manorial Court Books as Darland Rock. A more romantic tale in the village has it that a boatload of people returning in thick fog, anxious about their whereabouts, sighted the familiar shape looming out of the mist and cried: 'There's the old darling!'

Lympstone has its share of smuggling stories and many of the cottages near the river have odd nooks and crannies where smuggled goods could be hidden. Some have spaces in adjoining attics, where contraband could be passed from house to house, while the Preventive Officer was enticed in the opposite direction! Two known smugglers' runs were at **Parsonage Stile** (**5**) north of Cliff Field, near the old Rectory, now under the railway bridge, and at Sowden End, south of the village, from whence goods were carried inland by packhorse. During the Napoleonic Wars, a contingent of the Royal Devon Artillery Yeomanry were based on Lympstone. They practised down in Target Bay, and later on, had their own Drill Hall, up behind the Swan Inn. Their band has an almost unbroken tradition, splendidly maintained by the Lympstone Band of today.

The present **post office** (**6**) and its neighbouring properties are on or near the site of some of the earliest dwellings. Near by are **Harefield Cottages** (**7**), over a hundred years old, on the site of the New Inn (!). They were built by Mr W.H. Peters of Harefield as a memorial to his wife, Mary Jane, as was the Peters' Tower. This has been bought by the Landmark Trust and beautifully renovated. It is available for letting all the year.

The Peters' Tower and disused lime kiln, Lympstone

Few fishermen operate from Lympstone today, though the poles for drying their nets can be seen by the Tower. Seine-netting for salmon takes place in due season, by those so licensed. The Boat Shelter, provided when the harbour was lost, and rebuilt since, is, however, well used, for storage and shelter in winter, and by the Lympstone Sailing Club in summer.

Close to where the **Methodist Chapel (8)** now stands was once a boatyard, owned by the Bass brothers. Their wooden ships would have been launched from the Green, and timbers from this boatyard have lately come to light during the drainage works. Their house near by still bears their name, and indeed many others in the village retain the names of former owners, Hares, Mitchells' Staffords, White's Cottages and Metherells, for example.

Mrs R.H. Burton,
Lympstone Society

OTTERTON

The name Otterton probably comes from two Celtic words meaning 'water' and 'village'. The Saxons settled in the area around the late seventh century, bringing with them the open-field system of farming. To this day the main street is lined by farmhouses and cottages with fields divided into strips at the rear. At the time of the Norman Conquest, Otterton was the only village in Devon to have three mills.

Up to the mid-fifteenth century, Otterton was a fishing village, with access to the open sea 2 miles south at Ottermouth. There were no dykes or embankments, and in places the river is thought to have been 300 yards wide.

Over the last 900 years, there have been only three landowners. First, the Priors of Otterton: William I had given the Manor of Otterton to the Benedictine Order of Mont St Michel in Normandy. At the dissolution of the monasteries in 1539, the manor was bought by Richard Duke and it remained in the family until 1785, when it was sold to the Rolle Estates (now the Clinton Devon Estates).

The village was at its largest around 1850, when it was described as 'a long village on the eastern bank of the River Otter with 1245 souls and 3500 acres of land. Many of the female inhabitants are employed in making Honiton lace and two fairs are held here on the Wednesday of Easter Week and the Wednesday after October 10th.' At that period the village contained two bakers, two publicans, three blacksmiths, five boot-and-shoe makers, two butchers, twenty-seven farmers and five wheelwrights.

Most visitors approach Otterton by road from the A376, turning east at **Otterton Cross (1)**. This landmark, erected in 1743, has recently been restored by the combined resources of Devon County Council and the Otter Valley Association, so that the scriptural texts carved into the stone are once again legible.

The road to the village first crosses the railway (opened in 1897; closed in 1965). Then comes the three-span **bridge (2)** over the River Otter, built in 1836 on the site of a previous bridge.

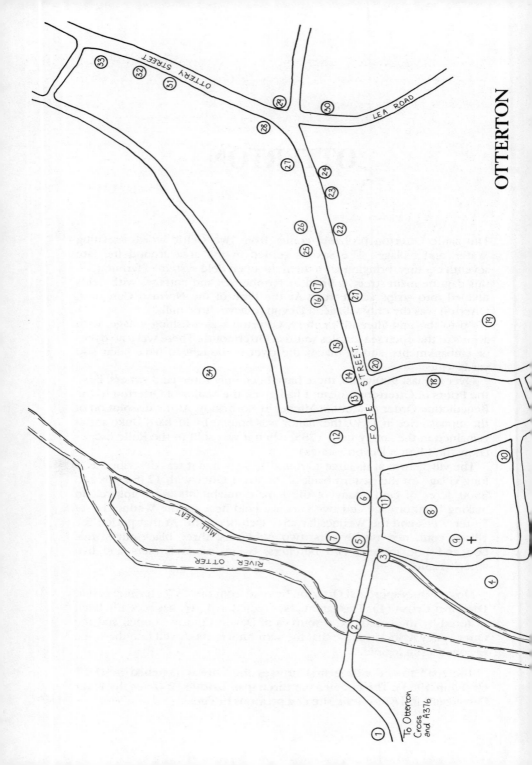

On the right is the car park attached to **Otterton Mill (3)**, which used to serve as a market for East Budleigh. Otterton Mill, fed by a leat cut in the early Middle Ages, probably stands on the site of a mill given in Domesday. It is again a working mill, the machinery having been carefully restored in the 1970s. It also houses craft workshops, a gallery and a restaurant.

Downstream from the mill stands **Otterton Barton (4)**, formerly Manor Farm. The present dwelling is probably a modernized version (1802) of a much older farmhouse. An early-nineteenth century painting in Otterton Mill shows the end of its Tudor building.

Opposite Otterton Mill stands **Mill House (5)**, probably constructed from several old cottages and later given a new front (c. 1785). To its left is a walled garden with a Tudor doorway in it. This is an unusually early use of brick in East Devon building. Between the garden and Mill House a wall spans the mill stream, probably the remains of a water-powered forge which once straddled the stream.

Mill House is on the west corner of the **village green (6)**, an open space famous for its chestnut trees, said to have been over 200 years old when they had to be felled in 1955. New trees were then planted. On the green also is an old stone flood-gauge marked off in feet. The old **Methodist Chapel (7)** on the left has been converted into a dwelling (Quail House).

Opposite the green is the opening of Church Hill. Climbing towards the church, you see on your left all that remains today of Otterton Priory, also known as Duke's Mansion House, or more correctly **Otterton Manor House (8)**. Above the porch are armorial bearings, now somewhat decayed; the building is used as almshouses. A north-facing Tudor window, looking up the valley, has had its panels blocked in, but its tracery is still intact. Several Tudor mullion windows survive at the south end of the west face.

St Michael's Church (9) was built in 1870 on the site of a much older church. The rebuilding was done wholly at the expense of Lady Louisa Rolle. Only the old tower was retained, later capped by a new steeple. The oak wagon-roofs of the earlier church with over 100 fifteenth-century oak bosses were lost; the sole surviving oak boss is kept in an oak chest in the church. The fifteenth-century font from the old church survives.

Walking eastwards round the churchyard, you will pass the site of another portion of the **Old Priory (10)** marked on old Ordnance Survey maps. Marks on the south-facing wall of the church tower show the line of the arches in the Norman church. Inside the farmyard of the Barton farm, on your right you will see two gryphons from the priory building, which have been placed on top of one of the Victorian farm buildings.

EED—E

The bridge, Otterton

Basclose, Fore Street, beside Otterton Brook

Walk down Maunders Hill. The school and its playground will be on your left. You will see part of the previously thatched cob boundary wall of the glebe close and the priory park.

On reaching Fore Street again, glance back at the row of **cottages (11)** facing the green. Built in the seventeenth century of cob and thatch, they form an attractive terrace; note the ornamental overdoors. The cottage with the bow-fronted window (No.3) was once one of Otterton's seven shops. Otterton Brook, which rises on Peak Hill, runs parallel to the roadway, and is crossed by several picturesque little bridges.

The first old house on your left is **Lawn House (12)**, within living memory a lace shop, operating the old truck system of bartering the lace-makers' work for goods. Then comes the **King's Arms Inn (13)**, rebuilt in 1889, and **Basclose (14)**, a medieval farmhouse with a magnificent lateral stack chimney added in 1627. It was restored in 1960. Next **Sunnyside Cottages (15)**, built in 1902; **Watering Farm (16)**, a Georgian house, said not to have been originally built as a farmhouse; and beyond, **Rosemary Cottage (17)**, the only ancient freehold tenure in the village, all on your left.

Opposite the King's Arms to the left of the butcher's shop is the old police station, now called Otter House, and the opening of Ropers Lane. A short deviation up Ropers Lane will lead you to the old cob-and-thatch **Ropers Farm (18)** on the right, and to your left, the **Old Vicarage (19)**, which has been turned into sheltered accommodation for the elderly.

Returning to Fore Street, the eastern corner of Ropers Lane is occupied by the **village hall (20)** built in 1923, the hub of all local activities. **Houstern Farm (21)** has another lateral stack chimney, added in the early eighteenth century, when, as in other Otterton farmhouses, an upper storey was made in the original floor-to-ceiling building. It also still has its cobbled farmyard and a roundhouse used for cider-making with a pony or donkey. **Otterton Bakery (22)** has 300-year-old ovens, now operated electrically. The **Thatched Cottage (23)** on your right is followed by the **post office (24)**.

Opposite are **Milson Cottage** and **Santasu (25)**, originally three cottages; **April Cottage (26)** was formerly known as The Gardens. Then follows a row of houses built in the 1930s to replace decayed property locally known as 'Rats' Castle'. On the left before the crossroads stand **Stantyway Farm buildings (27)**, about to be replaced by new dwellings (1987). The garage stands close to the site of one of the old **smithies (28)**, with **Cross Tree Farm (29)** opposite. Between Stantyway Farm and the garage was another lace shop, in which were found numerous bobbins, reels of lace thread and prickings when the cottage was first modernized.

Taking a short diversion up Lea Road (formerly Pig Street), you will see on your left an excellently converted linhay (a Devon farm-building combining a hay store with a cattle shed below). It is now called **Barn House (30)**, and forms an L at the back of what was once Cross Tree farmyard.

Turning into Ottery Street, you will pass **The Barn (31)** and **Rydon Farm (32)**, the latter with 'C.E.L. 1707' inscribed into the chimney-stack. Continue north, passing **Anchoring Farm (33)** on your left. Then turn left on Anchoring Lane and take the public footpath which climbs steeply and winds its way towards the Otter on a high contour. The hill is called Anchoring Hill and the field below is **Ferry Anchoring Field (34)**. These place-names have been much discussed; presumably shipping used to reach this point of the river before the estuary was partially blocked. From the high footpath you have a good overall view of the village and the arrangement of the fields behind the farmsteads. The path emerges in Fore Street at the King's Arms. Turn right to return to the green.

Otter Valley Association
(See p.18)

OTTERY ST MARY

'The most characteristic district of South Devon, the greenest, most luxurious in its vegetation and perhaps the hottest in England, is that bit of country between the Exe and the Axe which is watered by the Clyst, the Otter and the Sid.' Ottery St Mary is fortunate to be in the middle of that bit of country described by the naturalist W.H. Hudson.

Walk into History at Ottery St Mary

Ottery St Mary was an important town as long ago as the days of the Saxons, and as you take this walk you'll see fine examples of architecture from many ages. Certainly the best place to start is the magnificent **Church of St Mary (1)**, built in 1337. It is closely modelled on Exeter Cathedral and the interior has recently been repainted in authentic medieval style. From a gate in the north side of the cemetery you can see the Manor House, once the centre of life in the parish.

As you leave by the main gate to the south you'll find the ancient stocks in the churchyard and a small road running parallel to the flint-stone wall on your right. This passes the **Warden's House (2)** and the **Vicar's House (3)**, both part of the Collegiate Foundation (1337–1545), and leads to **Chanter's House (4)**, which is the home of Lord and Lady Coleridge.

Return to the church steps and walk down the hill, passing **The Lodge (5)** and **Barclays Bank (6)**, two good examples of the Georgian town houses.

Enter Broad Street and turn right into Hind Street. At the T-junction into Canaan Way note that **Cadhay House (7)**, a splendid courtyard manor-house of Tudor and Georgian architecture, is only 1 mile to your right and is well worth a visit.

Cross to the recreation area and follow the path beside the Anglo-Saxon **mill stream (8)** to Ottery's unique **Tumbling Weir (9)**, which was built in 1790 to supply power for the town's serge mills.

Looking towards the Jubilee Memorial from the churchyard of St Mary's

St Mary's Church from the Sidmouth road

Take the lane at the side of the **Old Mill (10)**, turning left at the end into Mill Street. You will see several interesting eighteenth-century houses, but please remember these are private and not open to the public. It is believed that Sir Walter Raleigh lived for some time in a house sited where Raleigh House now stands.

Carry on eastwards into Broad Street and Jesu Street until you reach the **United Reformed Church (11)**. This was built about 1688 and is one of the earliest Nonconformist churches in England.

Take the next turning on your left into Batts Lane and you'll see the **Lamb and Flag Inn (12)**. In days gone by a horse-drawn omnibus used to leave from here at 8 a.m. every Tuesday and Friday, bound for Exeter.

Sandhill Street, at the top of the road, was once known as Pigs Street, and if you turn left towards the town, you can see the seventeenth-century **Old Manor (13)**, which is thought to have brick-nogged timberwork.

Next on your left are two eighteenth-century taverns, the **King's Arms (14)** and the **London Inn (15)**.

Turn north now and walk up the hill towards the church, noting the early Georgian houses in Cornhill built around 1760, **Cornhill House (16)** and **Stafford House (17)** and **The Priory (18)** in Paternoster Row. This has been restored recently and rainwater heads bear the date 1719. Other houses in the Row (Nos. 17 and 18) date back to the reign of Queen Anne (1702–1714). It is said that the college clerics chanted the Lord's Prayer as they left the church each day through Paternoster ('Our Father') Row, and that **Amen Court (19)** marks the place where their prayers finished.

You should now be very near the church, where you first started your 'Walk into History' in Ottery St Mary. As well as the town walk there are many fine footpaths offering a few peaceful hours in the countryside. The Otter itself is a fascinating river and you can walk beside it to the north and south of the town. There are no less than 81 marked footpaths around Ottery St Mary; you will find details of these at the Tourist Information Centre, the Public Library or the Council Offices. There are also books at the local booksellers which describe walks around Ottery and further afield.

Ottery St Mary Town Council

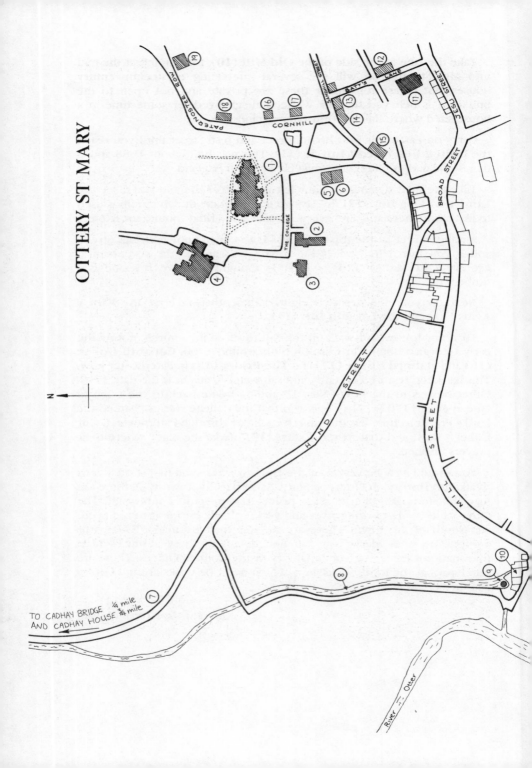

OTTERY ST MARY

PATERNOSTER ROW

CORNHILL

SANDHILL STREET

BATT'S LANE

JESU STREET

BROAD STREET

THE COLLEGE

HIND STREET

MILL STREET

N

TO CADHAY BRIDGE ¼ mile
AND CADHAY HOUSE ¾ mile

R. WKY ⸬ Otter

A courtyard opposite the church, Ottery St Mary

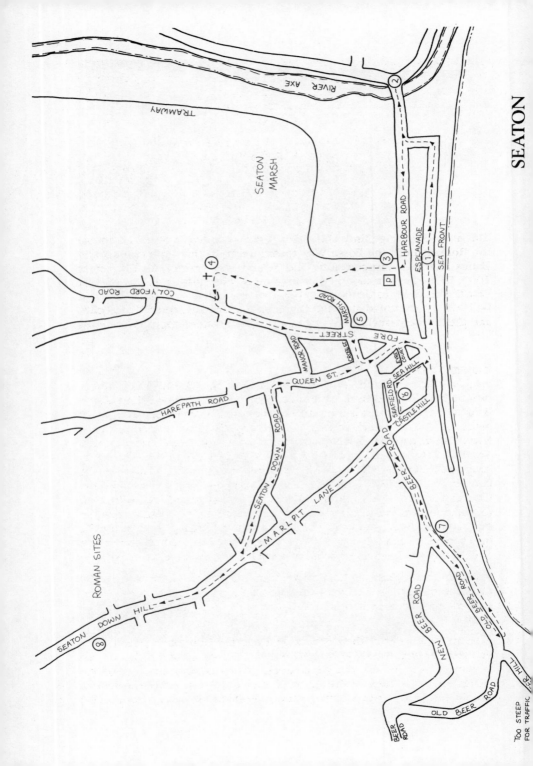

SEATON

The many Stone Age finds show that Seaton was active centuries before the Romans built the Fosse Way to Axmouth. In the tenth century the Danes attacked unsuccessfully and Seaton was granted its Charter in 1005. In medieval times there was farming, then fishing. It was the last East Devon town to develop: its population in 1850 was under 800 but by 1900 it had trebled. It is superbly set between chalk and red marl cliffs and the medical world used to praise its pure water supply and bracing air.

Town Trail

From the sea front go along East Walk, past the **Burrow (1)**, where beached coal barges used to unload, the coal yard being where Lloyds Bank stands. After this is a mound surmounted by a shelter. This was a medieval defence work and in 1544 Henry VIII came to see his 'New Fort'. This was wooden, with a cannon at each side. At the eastern end is Trevelyan Road, with interesting houses. Turn right at the bottom, to **Axmouth Bridge (2),** the oldest surviving concrete bridge in the country, built in 1877. The little barrel-roofed building is the toll-house. On the harbour edge you'll find plants like sea aster and samphire, used to make pickle. From here there were twice-weekly boats to London until the railway came in 1868. The Axe estuary is a favourite bird-watching area all year. At high water the birds feed on the marsh, which until the fourteenth century was a wide anchorage for ships.

Return along Harbour Road to the car park, where is the terminus of the Seaton–Colyton Electric Tramway (3), an excellent way to see scenery and birds, as it runs beside the river, along the former railway track.

From the corner of the car park go along the Underfleet path, beside the part of the Marsh called Merchants' Roads (a reminder of the medieval port), to the **parish church of St Gregory (4)**, where the village once was. Built of Beer Stone, flint, and Salcombe Greensand, it is mainly fifteenth century, but includes stone-work dating from 1190,   69

1300, and later. On the south wall is a scratch dial and inside are monuments to the Walronds of Bovey and to Salt Officers; there were salterns on the Marsh. From here turn left along Fore Street towards the town. You pass Tudor Cottage, with a typical 'East Devon chimney', then the school, built by Sir Walter Trevelyan in 1860. Next is St Clare's Adult Education Centre, originally a solicitor's house. Cross the bottom of Manor Road.

Soon you see the Manor House, a seventeenth-century building with a Georgian front. The little houses just before the Pole Arms were once cow byres. Jasmine Cottage (fourteenth century) is a little further along.

Continue past the **town hall (5)** (1904), or along Cross Street, then left. The thatched houses and shops opposite Beer Road are seventeenth century with good Victorian façades. The shops in Marine Place are converted houses. One still has the front-door steps.

From the Westleigh, once a convalescent home, go up Sea Hill. At the bottom of the Festival Gardens is the post-war Czech commemoration plaque, while the clock tower above commemorates Queen Victoria's Jubilee.

You come to **Seafield Road (6)**: this terrace of tall houses was built for the holiday trade, the dormer windows being those of the visitors' servants' quarters. Go left, up Beer Road, past the crossroads, and you come to Check House, originally The Grange, said to have been designed by Ruskin. Opposite are two bungalows with a common entrance, modern examples of Beer Stone building.

Branching left is Old Beer Road and the first house is **Seaforth Lodge (7)**, once the home of the Dowager Lady Ashburton. Here Ruskin, Carlyle and his wife were frequent visitors. From this road are views from Start Point to Portland and at Seaton Hole Gardens are acacia and bay trees, remnants from Madeira Walk, which extended to here from the West Walk. (There is an interesting geological fault here, with red marl (Triassic) cliffs to the east and white chalk (Cretaceous) cliffs to the west, the latter representing a downthrow of about 200 feet.)

Return to Marlpit Lane and go up it to the top of Seaton Down Hill. Under the fields on the right are sites of two of the four Roman villas in Devon. Emperor Vespasian was here with the Second Legion. From the **picnic site (8)** you see Axmouth and the valley beyond Axminster to Windwhistle, over Hawksdown and Musbury, hill-forts of the Durotriges. Return via Seaton Down Road.

Turn right at the bottom in Harepath Road. A little way along is the Infant School (1840). As you return ponder the changing life of this little town.

70   **Norman Barns**

The beach, Seaton

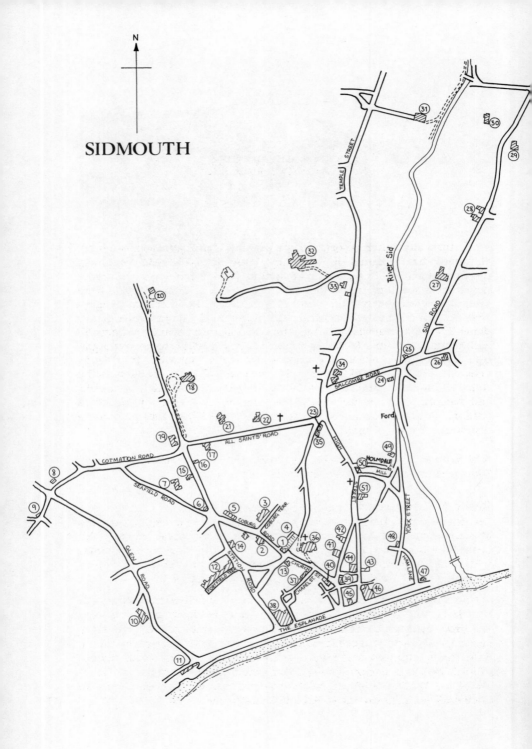

SIDMOUTH

SIDMOUTH

More than any other resort, except possibly Harrogate and Brighton, Sidmouth has retained its Regency buoyancy. The old port was discovered and encircled at the beginning of the nineteenth century by newcomers seeking elegant but rural retirement in homes copied from Walpole's 'Strawberry Hill Gothic' retreat at Twickenham. Lugar's *Sketches of Cottage Architecture* in 1805 caught the fancy of the gentry denied continental travel by the Napoleonic Wars. Sidmouth's architecture is primarily Georgian and Regency, with elegant wrought-iron balconies, tent-shaped canopies and trellis supports. Its flowing cedar-shaded lawns and white paint gave an effect of sunlight to the retired Colonial administrators and military men who liked verandahs and balconies and it became as popular as Brighton, but never as fashionable or gay. Its many handsome flint walls with gate piers are a distinctive feature of the town.

N.B. Sources differ as to dates, so those quoted here are approximate. Some earlier names of houses are given in brackets.

Walk 1: Regency Days (1½ miles)

Let us start in Coburg Road at **Hope Cottage (1)** (c. 1830), now the Museum, enriched by the contributions of many local people with beautiful old prints, period costumes and Honiton lace; a pretty house with a trellis porch and interesting windows with Venetian shutters. (Opening times are displayed in a ground-floor window.)

Continuing along Coburg Road, on the left is **Church House (2)** (c. 1812), with a notable Tuscan porch, large fanlight, spreading steps and iron balustrade. The old Free Library, maintained by voluntary subscription, is no longer here, but on the wall is the inscription, 'Come unto Me, ye children, and I will teach you the fear of the Lord.' Behind Church House is Barton Cottage (early nineteenth century), where in the 1880s Miss Cash, a cripple, embroidered names and monograms on linen with pink cotton; these became Cash's name tapes.

73

Nos 2–3 Coburg Terrace (1815), Sidmouth. This fine house was built for Sir John Kennaway in 'Strawberry Hill Gothic' style with crenellated parapets. The windows have Gothicized glazing and hood moulds over. Other features include peaked canopies with trellis supports, a common balcony with balustrade and an open porch with clustered shaft supports.

The White Cottage, Cotmaton Road, Sidmouth (early nineteenth century) has a tent-roofed porch with trellis supports. The earlier cottage on the left has two Gothic casement windows.

Turn right into **Coburg Terrace (3)** (1815), four handsome houses with a striking castellated parapet raised to form a central gable, and elegant windows looking over green lawns to **Amyatt's Terrace (4)** (1830), of beautiful proportions, set against a lovely background of Salcombe Hill and the church tower. At the end of the terrace is the Old Chancel, saved from the demolition of the old parish church in 1860, and rebuilt stone by stone with its fifteenth-century east window by a famous resident, Peter Orlando Hutchinson, and later added to for his own occupation. Returning to Coburg Road, note Coburg Cottage (Windsor Cottage), 1825, on the corner, with its typical trellis porch; then on the right a delightful vista of The Bays glimpsed from its gate; pretty Jubilee Cottage, 1810, and Olinda (Swiss Cottage) with steep gables and interesting windows. (Heydon's Lane, to the right, has some old cottages.)

Alma Cottage (early nineteenth century), thatched, has a trellis porch with peaked canopy and leads into **Alma Terrace (5)**, built in 1854 to commemorate a famous victory, pretty red-brick houses with striking white-painted windows and porches with unusual carved pediments. At Magnolia Cottage, with its beautiful magnolia tree and camellia, covered with masses of flowers every spring, cross into Seafield Road, with **Pebblestone Cottage (6)** (nineteenth century) at the corner. On the right are picturesque villas, notably **Littlecourt (7)** (early nineteenth century), with its unusual curved first-floor trellis balcony and tall sash windows; Seafield (c. 1840) and Seacourt, with elaborate carved fascia boards to the eaves, traceried windows and elegant first-floor wrought-iron balconies.

Note the beautiful carved doorcase on the side wall of Eaglehurst as we turn left into Cotmaton Road; the old fountain in the opposite wall is in rustic flint-work, and has a tablet: 'Sidmouth Parish 1850', a weathered lion's head and a shell-patterned stone basin. Further on are two beautiful thatched cottages, Old Cotmaton (Mills) Cottage (1830), with eyebrowed thatch and pointed windows, and **The White Cottage (8)** (early nineteenth century), with Gothic casements and typical tent-roofed trellis porch.

Continue over the crossroads and meet, on your right, the most beautiful council house in Britain! **Pauntley Cottage (9)** (early nineteenth century), with its domed thatched roof and pointed windows, was once the lodge of Pauntley House (The Marino), whose handsome grey roofs, belfry and cupola can be glimpsed further up on the left; it was presented to the town by Viscount Hambledon. In its garden is a large evergreen oak.

Returning to the crossroads, turn right down Glen Road with its lovely trees on both sides; parallel to this on the left runs the beautiful Glen 75

Goyle Walk, given to the town by Col. Balfour, containing flowering shrubs under beech and lime trees, with a new access from Glen Road.

Crossing Manor Road, on the right is the **Royal Glen (10)** (c. 1810, converted from an earlier house), in which the infant Princess, later Queen, Victoria lived with her parents, the Duke and Duchess of Kent, in 1819, and where the Duke died. It has delightful castellated pediments, a tent-roofed verandah and Gothic casements, with painted drip moulds. The front entrance has a good Gothicized porch, and displays the royal arms on a commemorative tablet.

At the end of the Esplanade is one of Sidmouth's most characteristic features: **Clifton Place (11)**, a group of charming cottages with thatched roofs and elegant windows almost at the sea edge. The first two are earlier (eighteenth century), with old sash windows, the other early nineteenth century; Rock Cottage, a thatched cottage ornée with pretty windows in Tudor style, verandah and ornamented chimneys, and Beacon Cottage, showing Swiss Chalet influence, thatched with carved barge-boards, interesting chimneys, pointed windows, and a good verandah and balcony. Further up on Peak Hill Road, Clifton Cottage, built in the early nineteenth century by E. Lousada, ends the group, which can be seen better – from a different angle – from the east end of the terrace overlooking the sea in Connaught Gardens; a marvellous spread of its many-gabled thatched roofs can also be seen from the side of the new bandstand.

Connaught Gardens were originally the grounds of Seaview, a house of sinister reputation, surrounded by a high black wooden palisade. The quaint castellated clock tower with belfry and steep steps down to the sea was built over the underground chambers of the old limekilns, and when it was used as a boathouse, boats were lowered from davits. After purchase by the Sidmouth U.D.C. in 1930, the house and foundations were demolished and replaced by charming gardens with lovely floral displays and a wide variety of flowering shrubs within stone and flint walls, delightful archways framing perfect views of sea and coast.

Returning to the Esplanade we pass the imposing Victoria Hotel, built in 1903 by Col. Balfour, and visited by many famous people including Earl Jellicoe, Bernard Shaw and Sir Henry Wood; Belmont, where the Duke of Connaught stayed, with its original 1820 castellated gateway; and Fortfield, since 1823 a famous cricket ground, but originally the site of a fort with four guns, built as a defence against Napoleon and demolished after Waterloo.

Turn left up Station Road to **Fortfield Terrace (12)**, of elegant Regency design, with first-floor balconies and tent-shaped canopies added later, built in 1790 by Novoselski but unfinished. Its houses became favourite temporary residences for noted people – Lord Gwydir,

Lady le Despencer and George IV – on a visit to the town. No. 8, the intended centre of the group, was occupied in 1831 by the Grand Duchess Hélène of Russia, sister-in-law of the Czar. The Russian double-headed eagle was mounted soon afterwards on the central pediment as a memorial. Elizabeth Barrett (Browning) also lived there with her family in 1832. She enjoyed the sea views, but found the round of crocheting and cricket a trifle dull!

As we end our walk at the museum we see on the right behind a wall **Harston Villa (13)** (Villa Verdi), built in 1820, with its balcony and scalloped barge boards. Here Lady Claridge conducted her school for genteel young ladies. We can also see the beautiful first-floor window and wooden balcony of the War Memorial Servicemen's Club on the corner of Church Street.

Walk 2: Around the River Sid (2¼ miles)

From the **Museum (1)**, walk west past the putting green, noting the large canopied iron balcony on Tuscan pillars on the side wall of **Church House (2)**; and the handsome central doorway and delicate wrought-iron balcony of Barton House to its left.

Turn right up Station Road, passing **Norton Garth (14)**, formerly the U.D.C. offices, with its wide trellis porch and handsome windows, and Belgrave (both early-nineteenth century), with its trellis verandah and tent roof verging on the pavement, and its eaves boards cut in trefoil pattern. Then we pass the modern but striking red-brick and stone archway of Fortfield Chambers (1911) with its ornamental drain-pipes (1928), built by Mr Hastings for Col. Balfour.

Continue up Station Road, passing on the left **Town House** and **Milestones** (Florence Cottage) **(15)** (both c. 1840); the latter is a typical Sidmouth house with Gothic windows, drip moulds, heavy iron flower-guards, ornamental barge-boards and a glazed tent-roof verandah. Cypress Place (early nineteenth century), has Gothic windows, drip moulds and a trellis porch. Tiny Gwydir Cottage, an old two-storey cob and thatch, and opposite, glimpsed through its gate, **Larbicote** (Page's Cottage) **(16)**, also cob and thatch, very picturesque.

On the right corner is **Audley (17)** (1810), which belonged to Dowager Lady Audley. It has stone gate-pillars from the old parish church, and, partly visible from the gate, an impressive portico with four Doric columns and a fine iron balcony. On the opposite corner is **Powys (18)** (c. 1820), a large house, originally thatched, with fine grounds containing many old trees. Large modern extensions have recently been built to provide flats.

Across the road is the fanciful and unique frontage of **Woodlands** (Old Hayes) **(19)**, a Regency frolic, originally a thatched cottage ornée, built in 1815 by Lord Gwydir, of striking appearance with its elaborately carved barge-boards and ridge-tiles, especially when floodlit at night. In the garden is a large Monterey pine, which flourishes as well in the mild salt winds of South-West England as in the Monterey peninsula of America.

Next up Station Road is Spring Garden, rebuilt in the early nineteenth century, with elegant porch, windows and screen wall, the home of some famous families. Further on is the entrance to Knowle, now the East Devon Council Offices, a massive Victorian conversion of the beautiful thatched cottage ornée built for Lord le Despencer in 1805, by Sir John Soane, the famous architect, and extended by Mr Fish, who filled its beautiful grounds with exotic birds, animals and plants. Many rare shrubs and large specimens of cedar and wellingtonia (Victorian prestige symbols!) can still be seen. Note the exceptional size of trunk and huge branches of the Monterey pine half-way up the garden path. Opposite is **Claremont (20)** (1825), with Gothic windows and striking balconies.

Returning to Woodlands, turn left down All Saints' Road, past **Cedar Shade** (Belle-Vue) **(21)**, an early-nineteenth century villa of immense charm, with shuttered windows under wide eaves, a trellis verandah and a grand Gothic-type conservatory. The garden contains magnificent beeches, a Monterey pine, and a large cedar of Lebanon. Here Elizabeth Barrett lived (1833–5) and fell in love with the minister of the Congregational chapel. **Green Gables (22)** has interesting steep pitched gables and scalloped barge-boards. All Saints' Church (1837) was built in Early English style. The **Unitarian Chapel (23)**, on the opposite corner, was the thatched 'Old Meeting House', Sidmouth's first Nonconformist chapel (1710, altered in 1884). Inside are an eighteenth-century pulpit, gallery front, and a clock dated 1767.

Cross High Street into Salcombe Road. There are nineteenth-century houses on the right (1–7) and Albert Terrace (1–4), some on earlier foundations; the rest are mainly mid-nineteenth century, with fretted eaves-boards and attractive windows in interesting surrounds. **Barrington Villa (24)**, at the end, is an early-nineteenth century villa with Gothicized details, interesting windows and porch, and an attractive rear view from the river. On the left Canterbury House and Sunningdale form a good introduction to one of Sidmouth's treasured open spaces – the Byes – reached from the bridge (1817), past a dignified **toll-house (25)** in classical style.

Continue past Mount Pleasant (Cote Lawn) on the right (early nineteenth century), with a large Monterey pine and copper beech in the garden, and up Hillside Road, past Brooklet Cottages, to see two thatched cottages: Salcombe Cottage (porch a modern restoration), and the beautiful Elizabethan **'Old Farm House' (26)** opposite. The handsome grey roofs of Salcombe Hill House can be glimpsed from here.

Return to Sid Road and continue past **Hunter's Moon** (Salcombe House) **(27)**, built c. 1800. A large Monterey pine dominates the drive, among groups of mature trees. There is a good central Ionic porch, a handsome parapet and small clock tower with a delicate weather vane. To the right in Redwood Road is a fine redwood tree, on the right about half-way up. Further on to the left are **Hills** and **Hills Cottage (28)**, with the great span of an ancient yew glimpsed over the wall, and on the right is **Sid House (29)**, late eighteenth century, with a good Tuscan porch.

Now we come to **Salcombe Lodge (30)** (c. 1810) one of the most perfect examples of Regency Gothic in England, in a garden with fine chestnuts, wych elms and beeches, a fitting setting to this architectural gem, its flat façade pierced with nine pointed windows and a low arched doorway.

At Sid Lane we turn left, passing old cottages on the left, and on the right Sid Lane Cottages (early eighteenth century, altered in 1840), and Sid Bank Cottages near the river, a picturesque spot. Turn left along the river edge, and cross the bridge, continuing downstream; then bear right across the grass and up the steps to **Woolcombe House (31)**, now Sidmouth Town Council Offices, much altered from the original ancient 'manor', but preserving the remains of its external chimney, and inside its beautiful medieval hall, halved in height by the insertion of a floor. The attractive thatched outbuildings form a pleasant group by the river.

Continue up the lane and turn left into Temple Street, with its two-storey old cottages, original sash windows and doorways. Further on is the entrance to Elysian Fields on the right, a residential cul-de-sac and 'planned development' of early- to mid-nineteenth century Regency villas, glimpses of which can be seen from the path in their particularly beautiful settings. On the right is Temple Cottage, now divided into Fairlawn and Lawn End (1826), with round-headed traceried windows, verandah and balcony on pillared supports. Next is **Sidholme (32)** (1826), a beautiful Gothicized villa built for the Earl of Buckingham, and the boyhood home of Prof. Lindemann (Viscount Cherwell), now a Methodist holiday centre. There are ornamental eaves-boards, traceried windows and a first-floor balcony with an elaborate Victorian cast-iron balustrade. Inside is a magnificent music room, neo-classical and rococo with painted decoration, where Paderewski played. In his father's laboratory in the fine grounds, the professor invented Lindemann glass, in the 1920s a major advance in X-ray equipment. Long Orchard (top right) (c. 1830) is a beautiful house with grey gabled roofs and handsome porch, ornamental barge boards, Gothicized windows and delicate wrought-iron balconies.

Returning past Somerton and Camden on the right, turn right into Temple Street, passing **The Shrubbery** and **Balsters (33)** with their Gothic traceried windows and carved trefoil-pattern eaves-boards, both

Salcombe Lodge (c. 1810) in Sid Road, Sidmouth, has Gothic casement windows with drip moulds over and elaborate glazing. Note the Gothic columned porch.

built in the early nineteenth century in the yard of a former farmhouse, which we next pass. Now called The Hermitage, it is a pretty house at right angles to the road behind a high wall, with similar eaves-boards and Gothicized windows. **Enfield** and **Radway Lodge (34)** (mid-nineteenth century), opposite, are of interest; they stand behind good flint garden walls. Radway Inn and the old shops are unchanged in their upper-storey windows, and there are old cottages in the lane to the left (Newtown).

Cross All Saints' Road towards the Cottage Hospital and pass **May Cottage (35)**, a pretty seventeenth-century thatched cottage restored in 1830, and used in 1885 as the first cottage hospital. Keep on along Church Path, noting the beautiful pebble wall on the left and the view of Coburg Terrace across the green. On the left is an entrance to Blackmore Gardens with its large Monterey pine, interwoven lime trees and a wide variety of oaks and maples.

The **Church of St Nicholas and St Giles (36)** was almost completely rebuilt in 1860, except for the fifteenth-century tower and two side arcades; the first church was probably Norman. A fragment of the original glass showing the Five Wounds of Christ was preserved by Peter Orlando Hutchinson and is in the Lady Chapel. The Duke of Kent Memorial West Window was presented by Queen Victoria in 1867. The carved reading-desk commemorates a famous citizen, Sir Ambrose Fleming, whose thermionic valve made radio possible.

Walk 3: The Old Town (1 mile)

From the Museum walk down Church Street. Somewhere near, Jane Austen lived and fell in love with the brother of a local doctor, who died of typhus, her first and only romance. The shops to the left mostly replace thatched houses burnt in 1927; others have been demolished. On the right look above the shop fronts to the old and handsome sash windows and drip moulds, then turn right into Chapel Street to Sidmouth's oldest group of houses (c. 1500). **Little Place (Littlecot)**, **Tudor** and **Merton (37)**, built of stone and cob with new slate roofs, and two projecting stone chimneys. Inside Tudor Cottage is a rare early painted screen (c. 1500).

As we go notice the winding course of so many of the older streets, giving the protection which the fishermen valued against the wind and sea gales. Emerging on the Esplanade turn right at the Riviera Hotel (c. 1820), once a terrace of three-storey houses, now with an added splendid bowed entrance. The **Bedford (38)**, (1805) was originally Wallis's Royal Marine Library and Reading Rooms, one of the first houses to appear on the front, with a 42-foot verandah, opened as a centre for rest and recreation in 1809, a fashionable meeting-place for all the notable people of the time. Enlarged from 1815 onwards and a top storey added, it has on its west wall in Station Road elegant transomed windows with drip moulds, a striking example of Regency style.

Returning east along the Esplanade, notice in the east wall of the Marlborough Café a small exposed patch of stone work from St Peter's Chapel of Ease, a port of call for the monks from Otterton Priory. First mentioned in 1322, it was used later as a harbour chapel and then as an inn, and was demolished in 1805.

Leaving the sea behind, continue into Market Place. The first **Market House (39)** (c. 1200) was replaced in 1839 and again in 1929. **Field's Shop (40)** dominates the left-hand corner, largely unchanged since 1849 except for the substitution of plate glass. Part of it was built c. 1810; note the handsome upper windows and one beautiful shop front with a moulded cornice and three carved heads. The Victoria Wine Co. was Mr Lethaby's printing works and bookshop, where his *Monthly Journal* was produced for many years. The unchanged upper stories are recessed behind the modern shop front.

In Old Fore Street note the **Anchor Inn (41)**, which may be on the foundations of a pre-Elizabethan inn; the present structure, c. 1840. Further on, early-eighteenth century two-storey shops, the upper floors still largely unchanged. Here beautiful lace was made for royalty by notable local ladies from 1830 until recent times. Banwell House has an old window and door; Hyatt's Antiques and the Little Shop retain original shop fronts, and Baskerville House the original doorway.

The **Old Ship Inn (42)**, restored in the eighteenth century, is reputedly 600 years old. It has 3-foot thick walls, rumoured underground passages and is said to have been one of the chief centres of smuggling in East Devon. Contraband was stored and pay-offs made until the mid-nineteenth century, and it remained a popular rendezvous and rest-house. The handsome doorcase has fluted Tuscan pilasters, a chinoiserie fretted frieze and pointed pediment.

On reaching the High Street, turn sharply right down Fore Street, noting on both sides the old two-storey shops, their upper sash windows mostly unchanged. They have interesting interior rooms, and Green's shop has an elegant doorcase. Boots is a new replacement of an eighteenth century thatched house, but the original rainwater head ornamented with fleur-de-lys remains. Opposite is Trump's store (established 1813) with its mid-nineteenth century shop front and flower guards; inside are some of the original shop fittings and mahogany shelves.

Knight's shop **(43)** (early nineteenth century) incorporates the two-storey 'Old Coffee Tavern', rented in 1881 as a reading-room and for the drinking of tea and coffee from 6 a.m. to 10 p.m., a rival establishment to the **Royal London Hotel** (London Inn) **(44)** opposite (early nineteenth century). This was an old coaching inn which became the hub of Sidmouth's social life. Its Assembly Rooms and card rooms, which would hold 200 people, possessed a spring floor, and for fifty years balls, tea meetings and musical evenings took place, and cards were played every night. The old coachyard can be seen opposite, behind an archway next to Knight's.

Before rejoining the Esplanade, on the right is tiny Dove Lane with some old cottages, and the Dove Inn, tall and narrow with interesting old rounded windows, a favourite meeting-place for fishermen.

At the sea front turn right to the **Beach House (45)** (c. 1820), a jewelled specimen of Regency taste, with Gothic windows, stained glass, scalloped open-work eaves-boards, delicate iron balconies with elaborate supports and a beautiful pillared porch. The Mocha Café and Prospect Café (c. 1805) were among the earliest Esplanade houses, and have elegant balconies.

Return eastward to the **York Hotel** and **Terrace (46)**, a striking example of sea-front development, the earliest (Nos. 1–7) c. 1810. Nos. 8–10 were added in 1911 in sympathetic style, and Nos. 11–12 (Carlton Mansions) were built in 1923 as Sidmouth's first flats and designed to complete the terrace. Each of these houses deserves individual study: all have beautifully different windows, original fanlights, balconies and canopies with balustrades and supports of wood and wrought-iron of many varying designs. Here were the 'Royal Baths' of hot and cold sea water used by the Duke of Kent.

At the end of the Esplanade turn left in Ham Lane; on the right corner is the old coastguard look-out, which was the Excise Office **(47)**, now the Surf Life-Saving Club; on the left is the site of the Royal National Life Boat Institute (1869–1916), with R.N.L.B.I. carved over a side door and an interesting old gabled window above.

Traverse the car park area, noting eighteenth-century thatched cob cottages with eyebrow dormers **(48)** at the corner of East Street, and continue north into York Street, old cottages on both sides; then straight on north past the car park towards the ford. On the left is the old National School (established 1821), now Potbury's Auction Rooms **(49)**: note the old Master's House with its wide eaves, interesting windows and door. Next is the gaunt-looking Feoffees' Almshouse, built in 1802 for a fifteenth-century charity foundation, and further on the remains of the old jail, with two high barred windows. (The stocks last used in 1804 are now in the museum.) Then comes the Old Mill House and Bridge House (c. 1830), with shallow box windows, an attractive group with its old cedar of Lebanon, overlooking the old ford and bridge, once the only route to Salcombe Hill.

Return up Mill Street, noting on the left the interesting gabled terrace with old sash windows, and continue right into High Street. A few yards to the right is an antique shop **(50)**, now the only thatched cottage left in the shopping area, possibly seventeenth century, two-storey cob-built with a new shop-window added. Opposite is a pretty cottage.

Turning back down the High Street, notice on both sides the mixture of eighteenth-century and nineteenth-century two- and three-storey buildings, mostly unchanged, except for the modern shop-fronts, their upper-floor windows of many differing types. On the right Peter Marsh, Burgoyne and Ladysmith House have older mid-nineteenth-century shop fronts, and Potbury's (1849) has a particularly handsome Victorian front with much decoration and striking doorways and doors with heavy scrolled supporting brackets.

On the left, the new National Westminster Bank is an example of modern development in an old setting. Further on we pass **Clovelly (51)** (late eighteenth century), its pointed transomed windows and door-case in original frames; Warwick House, probably seventeenth century, two-storey with old sash windows, and three old carved terracotta panels, now painted, above a late-eighteenth-century door-case.

Here we leave you, to wander at your will in the little side streets of this lovely seaside town.

OTHER HOUSES OF INTEREST (not on the map)
1. Continue north along Temple Street, bearing left at the fork marked 'Exeter': this becomes Woolbrook Road. Turn right into Manstone Lane, then left at the sign 'Tyrrell Mead Estate'. (Near the turning is the thatched and shuttered (Ivy) Cottage, early nineteenth century). A little distance up is **Manstone Old House**, probably the oldest residence in Sidmouth, dated 1389 on an external stone chimney. This is a two-storey medieval house with rubble walls of mixed local stone; the south-east gable is original with octagonal chimney-pots, and there is a pointed arched doorway with ancient sculptured heads which may be part of an attached chapel. Inside, on the first floor, is the 'solar' or upper room, with fifteenth-century windows and original beams supporting the roof. There are also interesting four-centred chimney-pieces and some old linenfold panelling.

Returning to Woolbrook Road, continue north, and on the left is **Lower Woolbrook Farm** (seventeenth/eighteenth century), two-storey cob and thatch with external chimney-stacks. Further on is **The Square**,

Ice House Lane (on the left), a delightful rural group of thatched cottages around a small green, eighteenth century or earlier.

Further along the road are other thatched houses and farms.

2. Continue along **Sid Road**, past Sid Lane. This is a pleasant rural walk with views of the valley and some seventeenth- and eighteenth-century thatched farmhouses and cottages.

Sid Vale Association/Sidmouth Town Council

View across the Exe to Topsham

TOPSHAM

Topsham has been a port since the days of the Romans. The buildings reflect its prosperity due to seafaring trades which have been its principal activity over the centuries.

Topsham can be reached by train from Exeter Central Station or Exmouth and by bus routes T from Exeter and 356 and 357 from Exeter and Exmouth.

Visitors coming by car are strongly advised to leave their cars in the large shoppers' car parks off Nelson Close and Holman Way.

The suggested walks are as follows:

1   Starting down Follet Road towards the river, along Ferry Road to the Strand and back up Fore Street. (Approximate time: 30–45 minutes.)

2   Starting down Fore Street and along the Strand, back up Monmouth Hill, Monmouth Street, Monmouth Avenue, across Holman Way by the foot-bridge and along this new road to Victoria Road; down past the vicarage to the church, through the churchyard and down the steps to Ferry Road and back up Follet Road. (Approximate time: 45 minutes–1 hour.)

3   Down Fore Street and the Strand to the museum, then on along the 'Goat Walk' **(13)**, round Bowling Green Marshes, up the hill and over the railway bridge to Elm Grove Road. Turn left at the post-box to cross the railway track and return down White Street (via Globefield), along Church Path to the Church and back up Fore Street. (Approximate time: 1 hour–1 hour 15 minutes, excluding museum.)

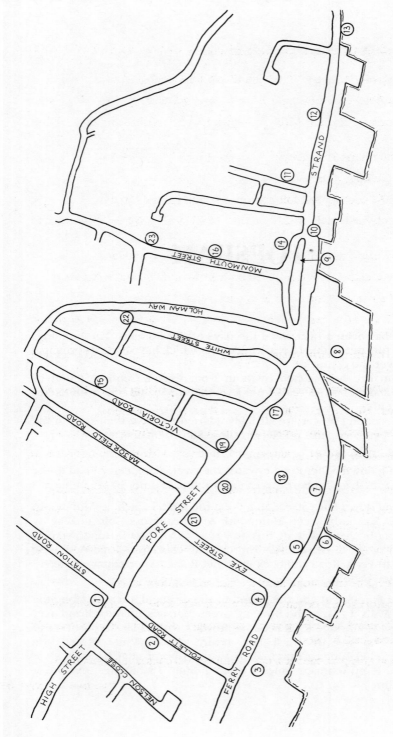

TOPSHAM

Key to points of architectural interest

1 **Broadway House** (1776); good wrought-iron gates.

2 **Clara Place**. Rebuilt 1841 on site of workhouse.

3 **Furlong**. Once a sail loft and shipyard. Figurehead on river end of house.

4 **Passage Inn**. Slate hanging on upper storey.

5 **Nail Cellars**, once a factory.

6 **Wixells**, another sail loft converted, with gables (1920).

7 **Churchyard wall** 1721; rebuilt 1843 and 1962 as described in tablets.

8 **Town quay** with quaymaster's house and King's Beam.

9 **Stone House**, 10 Strand; rainwater head and original window.

10 **Shell House**. Door hood with great shell.

11 **Topsham Museum**, open 2–5, Monday, Wednesday and Saturday; admission free.

12 Series of **merchant houses**, some with curved gables and enclosed courtyards.

13 **Goat Walk**, path along sea wall leading to Bowling Green Road.

14 **Retreat House** (c. 1700); porch and projecting window.

15 **Victoria Road**. Two groups of charming early Victorian houses.

16 **Monmouth Street**, a narrow urban street with terrace houses and interesting porches.

17 **Cromer House**. Eighteenth-century brick façade and good door-case.

18 **St Margaret's Church**; stone tower fifteenth century, remainder nineteenth century.

19 Seventeenth-century gabled houses and butcher's shop with ox head over door.

20 **Medieval house**; stone fireplace and arched door at side.

21 **Salutation Inn**. Fine gate below porch with large venetian window.

22 **White Street**. Charming group of cottages at top of a road of recently restored small houses.

23 Unusual group of cottages, odd windows, porches and plaster work.